the boy's book of
Indian Skills

the boy's book of
Indian Skills

Allan A. Macfarlan

GALAHAD BOOKS • NEW YORK CITY

Published by Galahad Books, a division of A & W Promotional Book Corporation, 95 Madison Avenue, New York, N.Y. 10016, by arrangement with Stackpole Books, Cameron and Kelker Streets, Harrisburg, Pa. 17105.

Library of Congress Catalog Card No. 73-81644
ISBN: 0-88365-028-2

Manufactured in the United States of America.

Contents

about Indian skills

This book salutes the first Americans and their way of life. That it was a good way of life is proved by the fact that, today, throughout the world, "modern Indians" of all ages try to live the same sort of adventurous, thrilling outdoor life lived by the red men when the prairie and woodland were green. Modern Indians make and wear the same sort of clothing as the Indians did, live in copies of American Indian dwellings, work on Indian arts and crafts projects, play Indian games and, as far as possible, try to copy the Indians of old. Indian boys, by their lives, skills, crafts and games, developed patience, courage, the power of keen observation, comradeship, sportsmanship and a sense of humor—qualities which are just as prized today as they were then.

The Boy's Book of Indian Skills is equally useful to adventurous boys, whether they are alone or part of a group. It suggests and describes in detail exciting, colorful activities which combine with and add up to useful, varied experiences spiced with fun.

Boys—and camp and club leaders, too—will find this book helpful in getting onto the Indian trail and following it to new and thrilling adventures in Indian life and lore.

No Indiancraft project described in this book is difficult to make, and no game is difficult to play. None of these crafts and games require special material or equipment. Nearly everything needed for these projects can be found close at hand, or can be made by exercising a little ingenuity.

The author hopes that this book will help to blaze exciting trails into new recreational territory—Indian territory.

chapter ONE

Living the
Indian Way
At Home and
On the Trail

WHEN COLUMBUS FIRST met the Indians in 1492, he
had made the navigational mistake of believing that the

Santa Maria was at anchor off the coast of the East Indies, so he called the inhabitants of the New World Indians. The American Indians have been called that ever since. By whatever name they were called, these reddish-skinned primitive people were related to the real discoverers of the land, who had trekked to these shores from Asia some 26,000 years earlier. The Spaniards, who came to plague and plunder the Indians after Columbus left, knew of his geographical blunder but decided that his term would do to describe these uncivilized peoples, who were foolish enough to fight for their land and for their rights.

The first settlers from England, 128 years later, owed their lives to the Indians, whose corn kept the Pilgrims from starving during their first winter in the New World. The new settlers learned much from the red men, including how to stay alive. All the early settlers' knowledge of how to live off the land came from the Indians. And so the white man, bent on a ruthless campaign to exterminate his former hosts, lived with and on the Indians, plundered their treasures, and stole their land.

These Indians who spread over the New World from coast to coast were fine, hardy, brave outdoorsmen who were able to live under conditions of hardship without losing their sense of humor and their lust for life. Their daring, eventful lives were lived on the vast plains, by the thundering sea of the Northwest Coast, in the forests and woodlands of the Northeast and Southeast, where they wrested a living from a hostile, arid land where white men could not survive. The northernmost tribes lived on the frozen sea region of the Far North, where the survival of the fittest was the rule. Other tribes lived happily beneath the sunny skies of what is now California until the coming of the white man. Indian tribes lived in the uncharted sea of grass which bordered the mighty Mississippi, while wonderful tribes—the Aztec of Mexico, the Maya of the

Yucatan Peninsula and Central America, and the Inca of what is now Peru—were Indians of highly developed civilizations, with cultures as rich and magnificent as that of ancient Egypt. The nomadic Maya knew almost as much as our best scientists know today about mathematics, engineering and astronomy. If Indian scientists and other wise men had known one-eighth as much about conservation as they knew about other sciences, these lands and their peoples would have flourished many hundreds of years longer than they did.

the Indian way of life

Anyone who is interested in Indians will find a study of these astonishing peoples rewarding and exciting. Many books divide the American Indians into classes such as hunter, farmer, fisherman, desert wanderer, and the like, but whether these Indians lived in tepee, longhouse, pueblo, or golden palace, we have much to learn from their ways of life and the skills which were a part of their heritage.

Before the coming of the white man, the Indians lived the sort of outdoor life that many modern people wish they could live today. Usually, they lived sociable family lives. The Indians of the Plains inhabited tepee villages, those of the woodlands lived in longhouses, and those of the Northwest Coast built magnificent cedar houses on the shores of the Pacific Ocean. In the Southwest, the pueblo dwellers lived in houses built into the cliff sides or in adobe villages, while other Indians in that region, taking advantage of dry weather, lived in crude shelters built chiefly of poles and branches.

HOW INDIAN BOYS WERE TRAINED

In most of these habitats, boys learned the crafts and

arts of their tribes from wise instructors. They learned to make useful and amusing things, how to hunt and play games, tell stories, run tirelessly, hike, wrestle, swim and keep fit, just as we do today. Indian boys learned to shoot with a bow and arrow, or throw a spear or throwing stick. True, they had more space and more time than we have today to practice such things. They learned the art of woodcraft, which covered many outdoor skills, such as living comfortably and skillfully in woods or forests and recognizing and knowing the habits of the wild creatures that lived in them. Without this knowledge, the instructors told them, they would never become hunters or braves. When hunting or on scouting parties, Indian boys were taught how to build rough shelters of various sorts which provided shelter from weather and the eyes of hostile scouts.

Though family life was important to the Indians, some of them, for one reason or another, decided to leave their bands or tribes and live by themselves. The life of a lone Indian was harder than when he lived with his people because he now had to depend on himself for everything he needed. Before, he could depend on his comrades to share their food when it was scarce, and it often was. Someone would hunt for him when he was sick, and his friends helped him defend himself from enemy war parties which sometimes attacked his band. Now, he was on his own unless he decided to return to live with his people. He had to learn to hunt and trap more skillfully, how to take cover and move like a shadow more cleverly, and to depend entirely on himself for protection against enemies from hostile tribes. His life was not too lonely, for he found comfort in the forest and, since his life was one of challenge, he was kept busy. He found pleasure in his skills and achievements and learned to live with hunger, heat and cold. He lived several lives in one, since he had to cook and sew for himself and learn new crafts by trial and error.

Today, many boys and men follow the example of these lone braves in various ways. They like to make things by themselves and find pleasure in lone hikes and fishing. Some enjoy these lone ways. Others do not live close enough to other people to be with them much. This book describes many skill-building Indian activities which a fellow will enjoy whether he is alone or with a few pals.

INDIAN TRANSPORTATION

Indians on scouting and hunting parties, even when far away from home for many days, had little difficulty carrying their belongings. Their possessions required for these occasions were few and lightweight and were carried in bags and pouches or slung over their shoulders or around their waists. Apart from food for the trail—dried strips of meat or fish and dried corn or beans, supplemented by wild fruits, vegetables and roots which he found en route—the chief weight an Indian had to carry was several extra pairs of moccasins. Tough as they were, these were soon ruined by miles of travel on foot over rough trails.

Travois of long, strong branches, cut into lightweight poles, were used in villages and when moving, usually to

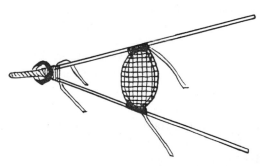

BLACKFOOT DOG TRAVOIS

follow the buffalo and other game from campsite to campsite. These poles of various lengths were fastened together with rawhide and were pulled by horses, dogs, or often by women of the tribes. Travois were common means of carrying Indian belongings such as tepees, blankets, skins, cooking pots, and other household and personal gear. On the plains and in some woodland village sites, the Indians used big animal skins or blankets to slide heavy gear around over the slippery grass or pine needles.

Of course, Indians who lived beside or close to lakes, rivers, or the ocean, learned to build all sorts of craft for water transport. These included simple rafts, the round buffalo skin bull boats, used by the Plains Indians, the

BUFFALO SKIN BULL BOAT

graceful birch bark canoes of the Woodland peoples, the swift, serviceable kayaks of the Eskimo, and the huge magnificent cedar canoes made by the Indians of the Northwest Coast.

COMFORT ON THE TRAIL

To Indians away from their villages, beds meant just about any place where hardy boys and men could lie down comfortably. It is wrong to believe that the Indians did not try to be comfortable whenever they could. Only a tenderfoot imagines that Indians, and outdoorsmen in general, enjoyed being uncomfortable. They did not! Indians used grasses, ferns and mosses as bedding and generally managed to sleep in comfort, even when away from their villages.

Lights were used sparingly by Indians when they were on the trail. Small, smokeless fires were used when needed for cooking or heat, and the torches required for hunting and fishing were made from the branches of resinous evergreen trees, birch bark, or cattails smeared with pine resin.

COOKFIRES AND COOKING

Cookfires were fires of various sorts built in safe spots and varying in size according to the needs and habitats of the tribes using them. All tribes started their cookfires by placing light sticks of dry wood on dry tinder. The tinder was very dry grass, mosses, and quick-burning barks. Birch bark was used when it could be found in the area. Over this tinder were laid small branches, often snapped from evergreen trees, and dry pine cones, when available. Small logs kept the fires burning for as long as required, and even when they burned down, a fine bed of embers and ashes remained.

Plains Indians, especially in hot, dry weather, cooked on fires built in narrow trenches or on patches of sand. Several women often cooked on fires built in such a long trench. Most Indians cooked on small but hot fires, making use of the hot coals formed by the burning wood of fires which had been burning for some time. Some tribes built fireplaces made of stones or rocks, while others cooked on a fire built between two green logs. Indians sometimes used tripods made from green saplings from which they hung their primitive cook pots, fashioned of leather, clay or even bark.

When food was plentiful, a big family stew pot was kept hot beside the cookfire and everybody helped himself when he was hungry. When times were hard and food was scarce, the Indians shared whatever they could trap or find. The Indians used the simplest methods of cooking, just as real outdoorsmen do today. They cooked food on wooden skewers by baking it in hot embers, and they boiled it in improvised pots, often made from the stomachs of buffalo and other large animals. The cooks of some tribes baked small animals and fish whole in clay. The people of the Southwest used earthenware pots a great deal. Today, modern Indians use some of these methods, such as cooking on skewers (fine for frankfurters, potatoes and corn), baking in the ashes and embers, and boiling.

COUNCIL FIRES

The council fire was an important part of the Indian way of life. These fires were used by tribes of the Plains, the Southwest, the woodlands, and the Northwest Coast. Important tribal meetings were held around council fires, which were also used as story and dance fires.

Here's how to build the log cabin type of council fire. It is easily lit and hard to knock over. It will burn steadily and well when taken care of by a good fire tender, and provides a fine, bright centerpiece.

To lay a council fire, mark a circle about four feet in diameter directly in the center of the council ring (described below). Scrape the fire bed down to mineral soil so that no roots can carry the fire underground. Raise the place on which the fire is built about six inches by stamping down earth or clay. The four base logs of the fire should be about three feet long and about eight to ten inches in diameter. There are about four or five tiers of logs, the logs in each tier being a little shorter and thinner than those in the tier below. Add tiers until the fire is about three feet high. Build a good foundation fire of tinder and short lengths of light, dry branches into the base of the fire and place a few larger dry sticks on top of it so that when the fire is

THE LOG CABIN TYPE OF COUNCIL FIRE

lit by a torch or taper from between the two bottom layers of logs, the fire flares up instantly.

The Indians used various sorts of wildwood tinders to trigger the fire. Among them were strips of dry bark (often birch bark), tufts of very dry grass, small dry branches of fir, spruce or pine, dry poplar or basswood twigs, and dry cones from evergreen trees. Because of the lack of natural fire-kindling materials today, they can be replaced by small balls of lightly rolled newspaper, short lengths of rolled newspaper which have been soaked in paraffin wax, and similar sorts of fire lighters which may be concealed in the heart of the fire to help set the council fire or campfire off to a quick start.

Council rings were built around council fires, and some sort of ring usually formed part of permanent and even seasonal villages. The rings were used for council meetings of the chiefs and as meeting places for the people, as well as for storytelling, dance, and entertainment centers in the villages.

Since modern Indians also use a council ring as part of their encampment, here's how to make and decorate a council ring and plan activities within it.

building a council ring

Council rings and fires can be built indoors but, as a rule, an outdoor council ring has much more atmosphere. The time required to build a council ring varies from a day or so to two weeks or more. Much depends on the site where it is to be built and how well-equipped and elaborate the finished council ring is to be. The inner circle of a completely cleared council ring should measure about thirty feet in diameter, with the front row of braves seated about three feet from the outer edge. The Indians often used such a circle with a small fire burning in the center, the braves squatting on the ground around it, and the chief or two who were conducting it standing either close to the fire or on one side of the council circle. Occasionally, a big log or convenient rock was used as a seat for the leading chief. Such a layout may be used today for temporary camps.

Place a wooden bench or decorated log for the chief and distinguished visitors directly opposite the main entrance to the council ring. It might be the only entrance, or there may be two entrances, the smaller one being close to the chief's seat and used chiefly for exits by individuals or small groups.

Council rings need not be circular. The author has built many good council rings in the form of oblongs and other shapes, simply because they had to be constructed on narrow peninsulas and in other areas where it was impossible to build a circular council fire site. The only difference in such layouts is the shape, since seating arrangements, fire, decorations and everything else is the same. One fine feature about some of the sites was the fact that a lake lay almost alongside one of these council rings, and water events using canoes could be staged close beside the council fire. Visiting braves disembarked and embarked right beside the council fire area.

SEATING

A more permanent council ring may be equipped by using fallen logs of various dimensions as seats for the braves. More comfortable seats may be made from planks, preferably hardwood, ranging from eight to fourteen feet long and a foot wide, supported by short lengths of sawn-off logs. These do not need to be driven into the ground if nailed crosswise onto the planks, with a log at each end and one in the middle. This is enough support for even fairly thin planks. A wooden portable chair can easily be built for the chief. A strong plank about six feet long and twelve to fifteen inches wide, nailed onto two or three stout logs, will seat the chief and his guests comfortably. If this seat is placed beside a tree, a crosspiece may be roped to the tree at a convenient height to form a back rest.

DECORATIONS FOR A COUNCIL RING

The finest decoration for a council ring is a setting which is surrounded by some trees. To give an Indian effect, a few brightly colored blankets or pieces of cloth dyed in bright colors and about blanket size are handy. These can be hung on poles or tied to trees, the tops of the blankets being about eight feet above ground on the outer edge of the council ring.

Colorful shields painted with Indian designs make fine, inexpensive decorations for any council ring. They can measure from twelve to fifteen inches in diameter and are set up either on tripods, as illustrated in Chapter 3, or fastened onto convenient trees on the outer edge of the council fire circle. To find out how to make these shields, dress for council fire ceremonies, and plan and carry out activities for council fires, see Chapters 2, 3, 4, and 8.

chapter
TWO

Dressing
Like
Red
Men

IN THE EARLY days of the unspoiled red men, before the white men came, an American Indian man was well-dressed, graceful, and unencumbered, wearing only a breechclout and moccasins. With the coming of the white men, new and unsuitable items of clothing were added to the Indians' attire. Garments such as trousers, vests, and Glengarry bonnets were adapted by the Indians to suit their ideas of prairie fashion. These needless additions are too often seen today when modern Indians assemble on occasions such as Indian days, rallies, and council fires. Once the dignity of Indian dress is lost, what remains appears rather tawdry. The notes on Indian dress which follow include some of the modern clothing, but those who wish to appear as authentic red men do not need to wear them.

breechclouts

Indian clothing was made from the hides of various animals.

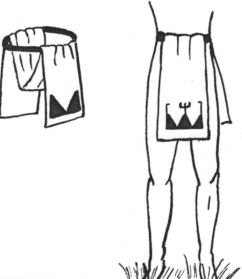

BREECHCLOUTS

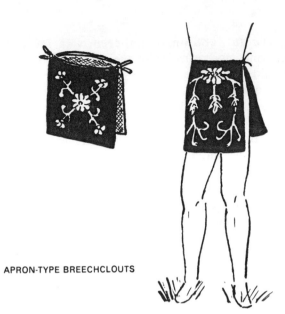

APRON-TYPE BREECHCLOUTS

Like most Indian clothing, breechclouts were different in the various habitats. Replicas of breechclouts of the Plains and some other areas may be made from real or imitation leather or cloth of various kinds. Beige is a good color. The decorations, usually on the front only, can be appliquéd, beaded, or painted onto the cloth. Breechclouts are worn over a belt at the front and back, as illustrated, and can be made from a strip of cloth a foot wide and five or six feet long, depending on the height of the wearer. They should not be fringed.

APRON-TYPE BREECHCLOUTS

The Woodland apron-type breechclout was made of deer hide or dark cloth, often black. It can be made from two squares of cloth about fourteen inches square, depending on the size of the wearer. These two squares are tied together at the hips. Both aprons were decorated with different Woodland designs beaded or painted on them.

They should be worn with long leggings or trousers, or over snug-fitting colored undershorts. Woodland aprons are not fringed, and are usually bound all around.

leggings

Leggings of various sorts were worn by different tribes, the decorations indicating the various habitats of the wearers. A popular sort, worn by a number of tribes, was made from buckskin or other leather, fringed or beaded. Practically all leggings were worn with breechclouts. They were convenient, saved time because no leg paint was needed, and looked very well in council.

Leggings can be made today from tough cotton cloth, canvas or other strong cloth, either dyed beige to look like buckskin or black or dark blue. The leggings of Plains and some other tribes were narrow at the foot, though fairly wide at the top. The mark of some Woodland Indians was the beaded or otherwise decorated cuff and a short fringe on the lower third of the leggings.

A useful finishing touch to modern leggings is the ornamental strip down the side of each. These beaded, painted

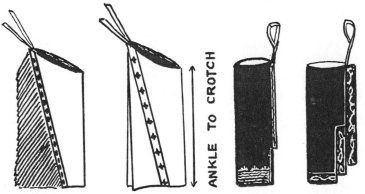

TWO PLAINS LEGGINGS (LEFT) AND TWO WOODLAND LEGGINGS (RIGHT)

or appliqué strips, ranging in width from one to two and a half inches, are usually sewn on before the leggings are stitched together. The leggings are supported by the belt.

anklets

Indians used anklets of many sorts, made of various materials and decorated in a dozen different ways. Anklets with small bells, metal cones, or other noise-making devices were worn by dancers, though some Indians wore them on

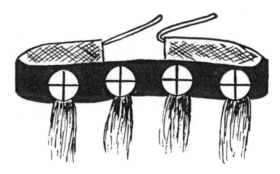

BELLED DANCE ANKLET

special occasions as decoration. In the days when metal tinklers were unknown to the Indians, dancers wore the dewclaws of deer to produce a rattling noise while they danced. Anklets were worn just above the ankle bones and the decorations hung down so that they brushed the tops of the moccasins. This kept them from being soiled easily.

Anklets can be made from strips of soft leather or brightly colored cloth from 2 to 3 inches wide and long enough to tie or lace around the ankle. They may be decorated with tufts of hair, natural-colored or dyed, beaded designs, or hanging strips of varicolored cloth. The fetlock type of anklet, illustrated, is most decorative. The Indians made it

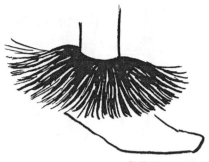

THE FETLOCK TYPE OF ANKLET

from strips of Angora goatskin, 2 or 3 inches wide, depending on the length of the goat hair. These anklets look particularly well in white. Wool yarn of various colors may be used to imitate these anklets, the wool being cut in about 8-inch lengths, doubled over a soft leather lace or tape, and sewn on at the top or tied in tufts which hang closely together. The hair or wool on these anklets should ripple and flow with the movements of the wearer, and care should be taken to get this graceful effect when making the anklets. No decorations were worn on top of these white Angora anklets, though sometimes dancers wore small bells attached to a thin, soft cord under them.

garters

Garters were another form of decoration used by the Indians. They were worn just below the knee either on the bare leg, when only a breechclout was worn, or tied around a legging. They varied in width from 1 1/2 to 3 inches. Sometimes they were worn as wrap-around garters and were made of gaily colored cloth, often decorated with tassels or short feathers sewn onto it. The Woodland peoples wore a strip of beaded buckskin about 3 inches wide with 6-inch tassels of colored wool sewn on each end, to hang below the garter.

Today, it is best to avoid looking too dressed up. When anklets or leggings are worn, fancy garters are not needed. It is possible to look very much like the real Indians of old by using replicas of authentic Indian dress, but once decoration is overdone, the best effect is lost.

moccasins

A pair of moccasins made the American Indian way is both useful and decorative. They are equally useful in the forest, in a canoe, in camp, and around home.

First, make a pattern by folding a 9- by 12-inch sheet of paper in half lengthwise and place the left foot, indicated by the dotted lines in step 1, on it. The foot should be 1/4 inch from the center fold and the heel 1 inch from the end of the paper. With a soft pencil, draw around the foot. Draw another outline, as shown by the solid line in step 1, 1/4 inch outside the first. At point A, which is the widest part of the foot, draw a line straight back to the end of the paper.

The folded paper is cut from point B along the outside line all the way to point C. When the pattern is opened out flat, both halves will be alike.

This is the pattern for one foot. Now, trace around it

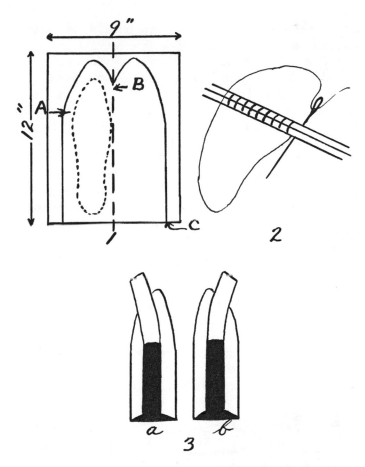

STEPS IN MAKING MOCCASINS

and cut out another identical pattern for the other foot. Put the opened patterns on leather. Trace around them with a soft pencil or crayon; then cut them out. Don't worry about left or right. So far, there is none.

Now start working on one of the cut out moccasins. Fold the smooth sides of the leather inside. Be sure to keep the edges of the leather even with each other. From point B, punch four to eight holes 1/8 inch apart and about 1/16 inch from the edge. Sew them together with strong beeswaxed or heavy nylon thread, using an overhand stitch, shown in step 2. The work will be neater if only four or eight holes are punched at a time and sewn before punching more. When the sewing job is completed, turn the moccasin inside out and press the seam with a hard, smooth object to flatten it out.

Place the moccasin flat, as in step 3a, and make two parallel vertical cuts about 4 to 4 1/2 inches long and 2 inches apart. Now, place the other moccasin in reverse position before cutting it, as in step 3b, so that it will fit the other foot. When the sewing has been done on both moccasins, try each on, slipping the foot well down into the toe. Wear the same weight socks you intend to wear when using the moccasins. Press the leather together at the heel, and mark the curve of the heel with pencil on one half of the leather; then mark another line 1/4 inch outside the first line. Trim off the extra leather along this outside line, fold the moccasin and trim the other side like the first.

Now fold the moccasin down the center of the sole so

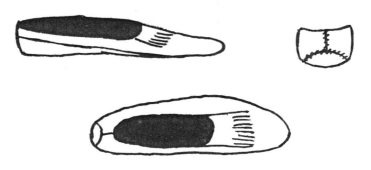

FINISHED MOCCASIN
TOP: side and back views. BOTTOM: top view.

that the top edges meet evenly. Make a 3/4-inch slit parallel to the folded sole and 3/4 inch above it; then trim the resulting little flap. (Remember to turn the moccasin inside out to sew it, as before.) Then sew the little flap to the heel, both inside and outside, to reinforce it. An old rubber ball or a darner used inside the heel. makes it easier to punch the holes.

Trim the tongue to the desired length or cover it with an outside piece of leather. It may be slightly wider at the end if desired.

These moccasins may be decorated with an Indian design and the tongue may be fringed. It is best to wear inner soles inside the moccasins to protect the feet from bruises, if worn on rough ground outdoors.

shirts

Though a few of the Indians wore shirts and leggings made of leather, shirts became a part of the red man's dress only after the coming of the white man. Then shirts became more and more elaborate and decorative. Deerskin shirts had few or no decorations for everyday wear. For special occasions such as war, ceremonies, and council fire wear, magnificent shirts were lavishly ornamented, often on front, back, and both sleeves, with quills, beading, painted designs, and fringes.

Though the basic pattern was practically the same, there were considerable differences in the cut and styling of shirts worn by the Indians of various habitats, such as the Plains, Woodland, Southwest, and Northwest Coast tribes. The Woodland shirt was often worn with a beaded belt. Some other Indians wore poncho-type shirts, open at the sides and often with open sleeves, but the Apaches, among others, laced the open sleeves together with leather thongs. The first shirts worn by the Indians after the white men came were made from practically any material that

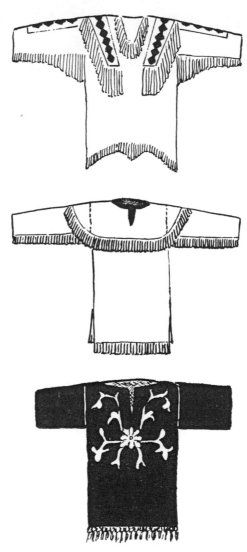

INDIAN SHIRTS
TOP: Woodland fringed. CENTER: Plains fringed and beaded.
BOTTOM: Woodland beaded ceremonial.

resourceful women of the tribes could find in the village. Such material ranged from cloth sacks to elk hides and beautifully dressed buckskin.

.These shirts can be fashioned for everyday and ceremonial use without much trouble. An old shirt, preferably white, may be dyed as the base for any shirt. Ambitious braves and those who are handy with a needle and thread can make very Indian-like shirts from flannel, which looks like buckskin, or unbleached muslin or heavy cotton. A loose-fitting everyday shirt makes a fine pattern. When the shirt is finished but before the decorations are sewn on, it may be dyed beige or ecru to give it that buckskin look. For the more elaborate shirts, strips of chamois or suitable closely woven cloth may be made into fringes coming from the top of each shoulder to about one-third of the way to the waist on both front and back of the shirt. The same sort of fringe may be used to decorate the lower part of the sleeves and the foot of the shirt. In the case of a really striking and beautiful shirt such as those worn proudly by the Sioux and Blackfoot of the Plains, the decorations can be a work of art. To make such a shirt takes time and patience, however.

The decorations may be beadwork, using sewn-on strips of colored beads to avoid much time spent on single-bead work, or the decorations may be painted strips of cloth or leather sewn onto the shirt. Though the Woodland Indians usually wore a beaded belt and beaded garters with their shirts, the Indians of other habitats did not. The illustrations will serve as models for Indian shirts.

vests

Both Plains and Woodland Indians saw the white men wearing vests and made artistic copies of them. These somewhat recent additions to Indian costumes were made of buckskin, other lightweight leather, or even cloth. They were

INDIAN VESTS
LEFT: Woodland. RIGHT: Plains.

shaped as shown in the drawing, opened in front, and laced in two or three places with leather thongs or brightly colored tapes. These vests were either beaded in bright colors or painted with Woodland or Plains designs, according to the habitat. Such vests can easily be made from suede, suede cloth or other material by using a regular vest as a pattern and working the decorations onto the finished vest. Real leather should be bound so it will keep its shape better. All vests should fit loosely.

ponchos

A poncho of the sort worn by some Indian tribes is a very useful thing to have handy for rainy days. It's easy to look like an Indian by wearing a poncho decorated with tribal designs and a pair of old blue jeans. The poncho can be made from heavy cotton cloth, canvas, an old blanket, a piece of tough plastic, or even sackcloth, cut to the proper size.

headdresses

The Indians dressed not only to meet the conditions of woodland, plain and forest, but also for ceremonial occa-

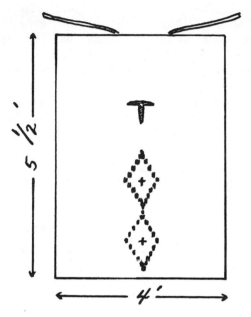

PONCHO

sions on which the dress of the chiefs was truly magnificent. Those who had the right to wear striking decorations such as coup feathers wore them on festive and ceremonial occasions. Among the most important items of ceremonial garb was the headdress. The Indians wore many kinds of headdresses, ranging from a single eagle feather to the elaborate feathered war bonnets of the Plains Indians, which are now copied and worn by many other tribes who really have no right to wear them.

For those who do not have the necessary materials or the time to find and assemble them, it may be well to consider the partly made kits for making all kinds of headdresses. These are sold by various Indian supplies stores, most big toy stores and many department stores. In the better kits the materials are very good. Of course, as boys learn more about Indian dress, they can change or perhaps add to the decorations found in the headdress kits. The feathers in the Plains war bonnet kits are imitation eagle feathers made from turkey wing and tail feathers, about a foot long, with the necessary feather base "fluffies" and decorations. Complete instructions come with each headdress kit and they are easy to assemble. Other headdress kits of the feather crest, roach, Apache, and Woodland types are also available at prices based on the quality of the materials. About ten dollars can be saved by assembling a headdress rather than buying a good ready-made one, which is likely to be expensive.

WAR BONNETS

Highly decorated, elaborate war bonnets of long eagle feathers were worn by the Indians only on ceremonial and very special occasions. Many headdresses had coup and grand coup feathers (see Chapter 8), indicated by colored horsehair tufts, often dyed red, tied onto the ends. The way coup feathers were marked was a language understood by the chiefs of the Plains tribes. Bars and notches of various sorts also represented coups in some tribes. In the old days, coup feathers really meant something splendid. They were hard-earned honors given by the chiefs—not pretty decorations bought or self-awarded, often by an owner who hardly realizes the significance of these feathers.

Today, council fire chiefs should make sure that coup awards are granted for good reasons and that their council ring is not overrun by befeathered chiefs whose headdress represents fancy and not fact.

Though coup feathers were awarded sparingly in those days, some chiefs earned so many that it was impossible to record them on a tailless Plains war bonnet or even on a single-tailed one. In such cases, the single-tailed bonnet was replaced with a two-tailed ceremonial war bonnet. This was worn on special occasions by some great chiefs, especially Blackfoot and Sioux. Such imposing bonnets look out of place these days, and even the most feather-bedecked chief should hesitate to wear one of these war bonnets which recorded past glories.

Even with a good do-it-yourself kit, making a two-tailed war bonnet is too lengthy a process to be described here. Many Indian supply catalogs tell how to make these and other war bonnets from the kits which they advertise. The crown of an old felt hat can be used today as the foundation for a war bonnet. Indian headdresses which are more practical, equally representative, and much more easily made are described below.

One of the easiest war bonnets to make was worn by Blackfoot chiefs. Though the feathering and decorating on some of these bonnets was elaborate, quite a good-looking one can be made by sewing a dozen big feathers, side by side, onto a nicely decorated headband which ties behind the head. The feathers on this headdress stand almost

BLACKFOOT WAR BONNET

straight up. Smaller feathers may also be sewn onto the headband, or it may be adorned with painted devices of the Plains Indians. Three or four thin strips of fur or brightly colored cloth about 1 inch wide and 3 or 4 inches long may hang from each side of the headband as a finishing touch.

ROACHES

These decorative headdresses were worn chiefly by Indians of the eastern woodlands. They were made of deer tails or porcupine hairs. These roaches are difficult to make nowadays without the use of roach kits sold at Indian supply stores. The main difficulty in making a worthwhile roach is the bending and tying of the sisal, other fiber or horsehair in bunches to the length of waxed cord which

ROACH

holds it evenly in place on top of the wooden stick or roll of cloth or leather which shapes the roach. The brow band may be covered with a bead strip, a strip of fur, or painted decoration.

ROSETTE HEADDRESS

A type of headdress worn by a number of tribes can be

ROSETTE HEADDRESS

made easily by sewing a single long feather onto the middle of a well-decorated rosette which is attached to the head-band at the back of the head. If a brave wishes to make the feather more attractive, he may tie a few "fluffies" (downy feathers) onto the quill just above the headband or on the center of the rosette.

INDIAN HAIRDOS

Most Indians had long, black hair. They parted it to braid it, often in two braids which hung in front of the shoulders. Sometimes one braid hung down at the back of the head. Modern Indians with short hair have to use improvised black wigs or purchase inexpensive ones where they buy their Indian handicraft supplies. Such wigs are made of imitation hair; otherwise they would be quite expensive. It's possible to improvise wigs from black wool by braiding enough strands of the desired length to make a fairly heavy braid. Two or more of these braids may be sewn onto the headband of most headdresses, and when well placed, the effect is quite Indian-like. Mohair can also be used for making braids, but it is not very durable. Some modern Indians make quite good-looking wigs from pieces of black, fuzzy material. A piece 36 inches long and about 15 inches wide will make a nice wig. The cloth

INDIAN HAIRDOS

should have shirring along the center to form the center part of the wig and to give shape to it. Fit the center of the length of cloth over the center of the head like a bathing cap, and make the braids from the material hanging down on either side below chin level. These braids should be cut into the material in the form of wedges, tapering from about 1 1/2 inches at the top to about 1/2 inch at the end. Such braids look more natural when wrapped with a strip of brightly colored cloth. A beaded or painted rosette may be tied onto these wrappings to add further decoration.

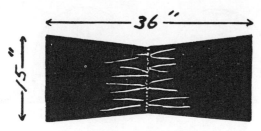

CLOTH WITH SHIRRING FOR MAKING WIG

HEADBANDS

Many brave, fierce Indians who had probably never seen a war bonnet fought, raided, and traded under a simple headband. Apaches and other people of the pueblos wore simple bands of cloth or leather around their heads. They

APACHE HEADBAND

were generally not decorated with even one eagle feather, though some had simple designs and a short colored cloth tie hanging behind. Such headbands can be made from a strip of soft, gaily colored cloth about 2 inches wide, tied at the back of the head.

A few tribes wore bands of fur, sewn into a sort of turban, with two or three feathers sewn on hanging down at the back. Sometimes the top of a turban was decorated with a small piece of colored cloth or leather on which a design was painted. These turbans looked somewhat like

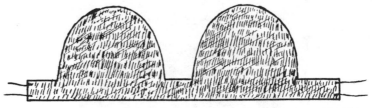

BEAR-EARED HEADBAND

the coonskin cap which Daniel Boone was supposed to have worn.

An unusual headband, worn by some of the braves of the Northwest Coast who belonged to a Bear Society, was one with erect ears resembling those of a bear. When these warriors did not wear the more elaborate bear head mask, they wore these ear bands when attending; their secret society fires. Such a headband should be made of fairly stiff gray or brown felt or other stiff cloth or leather, so the ears will remain upright when the headdress is worn. Fasten a short length of thong or tape to each end of the band so that it may be tied behind the head. The size of the head must be measured before cutting out the band and ears. Both band and ears can be cut from one piece of cloth. In a medium size, each ear is about 3 inches wide and about 3 inches high. It is rounded at the ends as illustrated. There is a space of about 2 to 3 inches between the ears. The length of the band is about 10 to 12 inches, from ear to ear, depending on the size of the head, and the entire length of the band is 20 inches or so, depending on the size of the wearer's head.

armbands

Making armbands is similar to making anklets. Armbands may be made of leather or any fabric. They are often decorated with beads or small tie-ons of brightly colored cloth. These armbands were usually worn about halfway

ARMBAND

up the upper arm, and they were just long enough to tie on easily without being tight. These bands were either worn on the bare arm or on top of shirt sleeves.

Armlets can also be made of pieces of metal, such as stainless steel, brass, copper, aluminum or tin. They are about 2 or 3 inches wide and 7 to 9 inches long, depending on the diameter of the arm. Armbands of this sort may be "stamped" when the metal is soft, or "engraved" with an ice pick. Beaded armbands look fine. They are made on a loom. Sometimes the beads are sewn onto canvas or soft leather with the lazy stitch, described under Beadwork in this chapter.

Very decorative armbands, known as arm bustles, are sometimes worn by dancers, but they are much too fancy for non-dancers. How to make dance bustles, the larger kind known as crows, worn just below the small of the back, is told later in this chapter, so any dancer who wishes to make a small arm-type bustle can simply make a miniature of the regular dance bustle.

wristbands

These were sometimes worn on one or both wrists,

especially by braves of the Plains tribes. They were made in practically the same way as armbands except that the decorative bands worn on the wrist were only about an inch wide. They were made of a strip of leather or brightly colored cloth and were decorated with designs or beadwork. They were usually tied, at the inside of the wrist, with the two ends of the band.

cuffs

Wide cuffs of leather, sometimes white, were decorated in various ways with beads and drawn designs in color. They were also sometimes made of cloth. Cuffs were a more recent form of decoration, adopted chiefly by the Plains tribes. Since cuffs flared like gauntlets and were

PLAINS CUFF

from 4 to 7 inches wide, they had more room for decoration than the armbands. These cuffs look best in lighter colors such as white, buff or pale yellow, with a suitable design of the Plains, Woodland, or other tribal groupings either painted or worked on each cuff with beads. Such cuffs were either tied on with two or three soft thongs or worn to fit tightly at the wrists so that no thongs were needed. Quite often the wider cuffs were fringed with buckskin or other leather. As a modern touch, copying the white man, some chiefs wore gauntlet-gloves as part of their regalia.

dance dress decorations

Before the white man came, the Indians wore dance decorations of quite a different sort from those worn by them afterwards. Earlier decorations were feathers, "fluffies," fur, fur strips, porcupine quills, dewclaws, bear claws, elk teeth, and other natural things. Later came little bells of various sorts, beads, sequins, circles and cutouts of tin and other metals, and colored cloth.

BUSTLES

The bustle is a rather flashy but highly decorative ornament, usually worn as part of a striking dance costume. This bustle, or crow, used to be worn only by warriors who had won high battle honors. The redoubtable tribal police, often known as "dog soldiers," were generally wearers of this hard-won award.

BUSTLES
LEFT: arm bustle. RIGHT: waist bustle.

The Algonquian form of bustle was made in a long oblong style from a piece of red, blue or black cloth such
as velveteen, about 30 inches long and 12 or 13 inches
wide. It was usually lavishly adorned with feathers, beaded
rosettes, or decorated disks. A thong at the top on each
side tied this bustle around the waist.

The Plains bustles were usually round, about 24 to 36
inches in diameter, the centerpiece being a circle of polished tin from which feather decorations radiated,
as shown. An easy way to make the round bustle is to use
a foundation circle of strong, stiff cardboard. Cover it
with a piece of bright cloth and paint designs or sew feathers of various lengths on it, starting with the outer circle,
and working toward the center.

ROSETTES

Rosettes were made in a number of ways and in a variety
of sizes. They may be worn on the backs of the wrists or as a
decoration on headdress bands. They are from 2 to 6 inches
in diameter and can be made of beaded circles of cloth

ROSETTES
LEFT: feathered. RIGHT: beaded.

or cloth circles painted with designs. The fancier ones are
made from one of these centers with small colored feathers
sewn onto the edge so that they radiate from it.

CONCHAS

Conchas are another form of circular decoration about

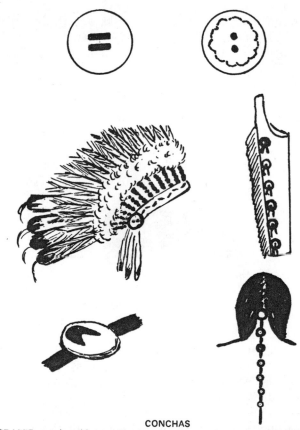

CONCHAS

TOP LEFT: concha with two slits through which a ribbon or belt can be threaded. TOP RIGHT: button-like concha with two holes, used on headbands, leggings, etc. LEFT CENTER: concha on headdress band. RIGHT CENTER: conchas on leggings. BOTTOM LEFT: conchas on ribbon or leather band. BOTTOM RIGHT: conchas on braid ribbon or leather strip, decreasing in size towards end of braid.

2 inches in diameter, worn on headbands or sewn on the front of leggings, four or six on each legging. They are most easily made of soft, workable metals such as aluminum, pewter, nickel, silver or tin. One must be careful that the edges are quite smooth, after being tapped flat

with a wooden mallet. When the disks are ready, tribal designs may be scratched into the surfaces with an ice pick, or the designs may be stamped onto them. Typical Plains designs are good-looking.

BEAR CLAW NECKBANDS

Bear claw neckbands used to be a favorite among Indian chiefs and braves who got their claws the hard way. They are quite easy to cut out of soft woods, such as white pine or basswood. First cut a pattern from stiff cardboard, as shown, and draw around it onto a 3/4-inch strip of

PATTERN FOR BEAR CLAW

soft wood. Mark the number of claws needed for the neckband (usually from eight to eleven), cut them from the wood, and whittle, then sandpaper them to the desired size. Paint the base of each claw, through which the hole is made, a dark brown. Then brown the rest of the claw by passing it through the flame of a candle without charring the wood. Smear the browned claw with candle wax, letting the soft wood soak up the paraffin wax. When the color of the claws is right, polish them with an oily cloth and allow them to dry.

The claws may be strung on a rawhide thong, string or cord, with a brightly colored bead between each two claws. Red and yellow wooden beads help to make a really good-looking neckband. For those who are not good at making such artifacts, an easy way out is to buy the plastic or wooden claws, ready-made at an Indian supplies store.

Most braves today are not as handy with a needle as the Indians were, so the easiest way for them to do beadwork is to buy a kit which comes complete with loom in an Indian supplies store. There are kits of various sizes and prices to suit the wishes of all who are interested in beadwork. For fellows who wish to do a little beadwork on their own, this is how the Indians sewed beads onto buckskin or cloth.

Though the Indians used sinews for beadwork, strong waxed linen thread or nylon thread is easier to come by these days. First, knot one end of the thread and sew it to the material at the starting point; then thread two to nine beads onto the thread. Pass the needle down through the material, as shown, then bring it back up, near the last

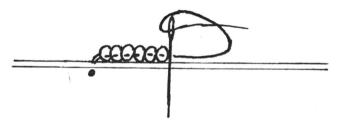

SEWING BEADS WITH THE LAZY STITCH

bead, and thread about the same number of beads onto it again, repeating the procedure until the end of the row. The thread must be pulled tightly each time it is passed through the cloth so that the beads will lie flat against it and not bulge. This is called the lazy stitch.

Another way, the running stitch, is similar except that each time the needle and thread is pushed down through the cloth and brought back up, it is brought up just before the last two beads and threaded through them before more beads are added. This process is repeated until the end of the row is reached. There, the thread is made fast and another row is begun.

Beadwork may be done on small strips, circles or squares of cloth which are then sewn onto the garment or decoration, instead of directly onto the object. This is much easier than working directly on a large piece of clothing.

chapter
THREE

Making Gear
and
Regalia
For the Tribe

THOUGH THE WOMEN of the tribes did much of the leatherwork and sewing, and some decorative work with porcupine quills, beads and feathers, the men, too, did a good deal of decorative and painting work. This was largely because of the secret totems and magic figures built into many of the designs. Such things were not only secret and sacred but also strictly personal, so much so that many warriors did not even tell their friends of trail and warpath what some of the symbols and charms meant. The wearers believed that to do so would weaken or destroy some of the spirit power possessed by the designs and totems. Such precautions were chiefly connected with a brave's personal belongings, such as his medicine bag or pouch, coup stick, shield, mask, etc.

decorative sticks and poles

The Indians used decorative sticks and poles for many purposes—to send invitations, to record great achievements and to designate ownership of personal possessions.

INVITATION STICKS

The American Indian invitations to powwows, feasts and council meetings were always honored by the braves who received them. Invitation sticks were often sent out for private ceremonies, such as naming a child, honoring a boy or an older brave, or celebrating success in a hunt. These were family affairs, but the invitation sticks were sent out ceremoniously, especially among the Plains and Woodland Indians. Hiawatha, a real Indian chief and powerful medicine man, sent out invitation sticks which were colored bright red.

Invitation sticks may be made so easily that a fellow may send out his own if he holds an Indian night for his friends. This is how an invitation stick can be made without cutting branches from live trees. A dowel stick about 1 or 2 feet long and 1/2 inch in diameter makes a fine invitation stick when painted and decorated. Usually the dowel does not need to be sandpapered. It needs only a coat of bright paint and a few tufts of feathers about 2 1/2 inches long, tied to one end of the stick. Instead of being painted, the stick can be oiled and decorated with stripes burned into the wood.

Various tribes used different lengths of sticks decorated in many ways. The Ojibway, for instance, used sticks about 12 inches long without decoration of any kind.

The sticks sent out for a council fire can be collected when the visitors arrive, or they may be presented to the guests as colorful souvenirs of the event.

COUP STICKS

Coup sticks could be called record sticks, since each feather, coup feather and other decoration told of brave deeds performed and of other worthy achievements. Often coup sticks were short, blunt-ended lances of various lengths, frequently used to strike an armed enemy. Coup sticks were

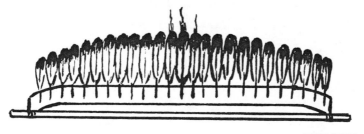

COUP STICK

MAKING GEAR AND REGALIA • 53

made in a number of ways, in various lengths, and with widely varied decorations. The drawing shows the usual form of these greatly prized sticks.

To make a coup stick easily, all that is needed is a dowel stick about 1 inch in diameter and 4 or 6 feet long. This stick may be painted and decorated with painted designs. The main part of the stick is a 3-foot-long strip of red flannel or similar cloth about 2 inches wide, attached directly to the pole or allowed to hang down at the center. The coup award feathers are sewn to the flannel by the quills. Feathers proclaiming grand coups are sewn to the center of the flannel band, as shown, and these feathers' may be longer than the coup feathers. Any big white or near-white feathers may be used as coup feathers and can be made to look like eagle feathers by painting or dyeing about 1 1/2 inches of the tops black or dark brown.

COUP POLE

A coup pole is a decorative pole which may be driven into the ground about 6 feet away from the chief's seat at a

COUP POLE

council fire, or set up in the open or before a chief's cabin. It is made from a softwood or hardwood pole about 7 feet long which is tapered so that it is about 3 inches in diameter at the pointed end and about 5 inches in diameter at the top. The pole is painted brightly in red with 2- or 3-inch orange circles painted around it at 8-inch intervals to about one-quarter way from the foot of the pole. When the pole has been set up, a long white feather, painted dark brown or black at the tip to resemble an eagle's feather, may be stuck into a hole drilled in the top of the pole. How this pole is used in counting and claiming coup is told in Chapter 8.

These days, when conservation is being enforced and poles are becoming scarcer and more expensive, the strong, thick rolls which carpets are rolled around make good substitutes for wooden poles. Since these rolls are only made of cardboard or composition, they should be painted well to make them waterproof and should not be left standing outdoors except when actually in use. A short length of pole, the diameter of the inside of the roll, can be driven into the ground and the roll fitted firmly onto it.

OWNER'S STAFF

Just as the Indians marked their arrows in different ways for identification, the Indians also used staffs or sticks of various lengths to show ownership of their tepee, when it was folded for transport, and other personal belongings. The staffs ranged from 3 to 5 feet in length, and the sticks, which were pointed at the end so they could be driven into the ground easily, ranged from 26 to 32 inches in length. Like most possessions of the Indians, these sticks were not only useful but also decorative. They were marked in many simple and fantastic ways so that there was no possible doubt as to who owned them. An owner might use only his personal totem, such as a bird or animal or an object which

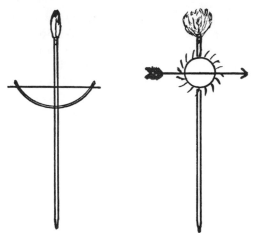

OWNERSHIP STICKS

illustrated his name. Another Indian might use brightly colored disks or shells; cutout moons, stars, or circles; strips of varicolored cloth, fur, or leather; or other means of ornamentation with a purpose.

making things for ceremonies and dances

There can be a lot of fun in making colorful masks, hoops and shields which played an important part in Indian dances and ceremonies.

MASKS

The Iroquois, especially Seneca members of the False Face Society, wore masks to cure the sick and drive out evil spirits. Masks were used a great deal in the Southwest. The Hopi used masks for various important religious and social ceremonies, and their kachinas, or supernatural beings, were always masked. So were the Zuñi clowns. The Apache devil dancers (medicine men) wore special masks which were fanciful and colorful. The greatest variety of

ARTICULATED DEER MASK OF THE BELLA COOLA INDIANS

masks were worn by the Indians of the Northwest Coast. They had masks for ceremonies, fun, and rituals. Some were beautiful masks with movable parts (articulated masks) and realistic beast and bird masks. Often these Indians wore complete costumes which matched the masks and gave the actors and dancers the appearance of the creatures being imitated. Masks such as those worn by the Seneca were partially carved from the living trees—basswood, as a rule, though willow and other easily carved woods were also used.

Masks can be made easily from cardboard, paper, corn husks, cloth, some cardboard boxes, and papier-mâché. It takes some thought and work before a mask made from any of these materials is ready to wear at a council ring ceremony, secret society meeting, or a dance. One of the easiest masks to make is formed from a piece of lightweight, flexible, strong cardboard. The cardboard may be rolled into a cylinder or folded into a boxlike shape open at both ends. Such spirit or animal masks, which fit over the face, are completed by gluing or sewing noses, horns, ears, fur, feathers and other decorations onto them. When complete, these masks may be painted in suitable colors with ordinary paint or watercolors.

The most professional way to make masks, especially grotesque ones, is by shaping wet papier-mâché (paper

pulp) in molds, or with the fingers, into the form desired. When the masks dry, they will be hard and strong. An easy way to make papier-mâché is to soak paper which has been torn into strips—newspaper will do—in water and shred or pound it into pulp. The pulp should be left soaking in water overnight, or it may be boiled to save time. When the pulp becomes dry, add enough water to make it easy to shape as desired. Mold this mixture by hand and allow it to dry thoroughly before adding the finishing touches.

HOOPS

Hoops of various sizes are a useful part of Indian equipment. They can be used for Indian hoop dances, playing various games, ornamentation, and as frameworks for decorative shields. These hoops were made in sizes ranging from 4 inches to 20 inches or so in diameter, and in various strengths. The Indian usually cut a branch, sapling or shoot of willow or ash of the right length and thickness. He then made it into a circle by bending it around a suitable tree or log and tying the ends together while the hoop took shape. The stick was then rubbed smooth and a join about 3 inches long was whittled on the bottom side at one end and the top side at the other, as shown, so the ends would

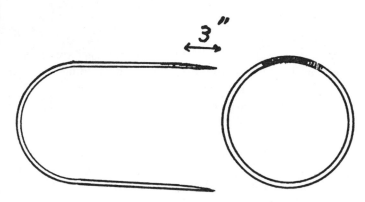

STEPS IN MAKING A HOOP
LEFT: a 3-inch join is whittled at each end of stick. RIGHT: the ends are bound.

fit smoothly together when joined. Finally, the hoop was painted in bright colors and sometimes also decorated with two or three short tufts of dyed hair.

Today, when woods and forests are becoming scarcer and the trees and bushes are protected, there are easier ways of getting hoops for Indian artifacts. They can be bought ready-made, in various sizes. There are wooden embroidery hoops available and aluminum and wooden hoops such as those children play with, as well as other sorts. Fine hoops of wood or aluminum, measuring from 20 to 24 inches, may be bought for Indian dance use. Those who wish to make their own hoops from scratch may use coils of rattan half an inch or a little thicker in diameter. These may be bought fairly cheaply at stores which sell arts and crafts materials and at places which make rattan porch furniture or weave baskets. The desired length is cut from the coil and bent to shape around a pail. Then the cuts are made at each end as described above. They should be lightly smeared with good glue or cement and bound tightly together over the entire splice or at each end of it with strong twine. After sandpapering and decorating, the hoop is ready for use.

The Indians made fine shields for protection from enemy arrows in battle, making medicine and warding off evil spirits, decorative use, and some dances. Like practically all of the Indian artifacts, these shields were well and strongly made as well as being beautiful. Replicas of these shields, which are not difficult to make but will look well when completed, can be made by modern Indiancrafters. Some ways of making these shields are better than others, but not many fellows today spend as much time working on a shield as the Indians did.

Decorative shields can be made in almost any size, from various materials, and in different ways. The easiest way to get a small, perfectly round shield of fine appearance is to buy an embroidery hoop. These can be bought cheaply in sizes ranging from only a few inches to over a foot in diameter. (For those who find it more interesting to make their own hoops, how to do so is told under Hoops earlier in this chapter.) They may be covered with real or imitation leather, canvas, coarse cotton or some other strong cloth.

Cut the material about 3 inches larger all around than the hoop and, to keep the shield cover taut, lace it inside,

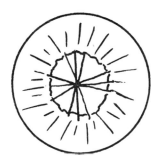

INDIAN SHIELDS
LEFT: back view. RIGHT: front view.

as shown, with cloth laces. Once the cover is in place, you may paint the material in any basic color desired. When the paint is dry, paint the designs onto the shield. A brave's totem may be painted in the center of the shield and other designs painted around the edges. The background color is usually yellow, white or beige to give it a leathery look, and there should not be so much decorative painting on the shield that the background color does not show up strongly. White buckskin, used as decorative shield covers by some of the Plains tribes, was very effective, with only three or four eagle feathers sewn onto the center of the cover and, sometimes, drops of feathers and red flannel hanging down from the foot of the shield.

Decorative shields may also be cut from beaverboard and the designs painted directly onto it. These shields may be cut in any useful size and are strong.

A shield ranging from 14 to 16 inches in diameter is a good size. It may be hung on a tripod outside a tepee or used as a dance shield. A loop may be fastened to the top

INDIAN SHIELD ON TRIPOD

rear side of the shield or passed through two holes made in the top of the shield and tied loosely at the back so that the loop may be used to hang the shield from a tripod or pole. Two thongs or wide laces should form loops at the back of the shield; through the top loop the forearm is passed, the fingers holding the second loop. These thongs may be glued strongly in the correct places on the back of the shield, or the two ends of each loop may be passed through two holes, 2 or 3 inches apart, and tied at the back of the shield, leaving a loop of the right size for the forearm and hand to pass through. When the holes are made directly through a shield, a decoration such as a rosette, feather, or concha may be used to hide the holes on the front of the shield cover. Decorations which may be used to hang down from the lower third of the shield are feathers, strips of brightly colored cloth, fur, bear claws, and horsehair. (How to make bear claws is told in Chapter 2.)

rhythm instruments

The Indians used various instruments to accompany singers, mark time for dance steps, or highlight dramatic events in the council ring. Among them were rattles, tom-toms and beaters.

RATTLES

Rattles are very effective and easy to make. A fine imitation of a turtleshell rattle can be made from a small wooden box. First, put a few small pebbles, marbles or round wooden beads inside the box to test the rattle for sound. Next, cut a hole in each end of the box. Push a strong wooden handle through the hole in one end and out the hole at the other end. Here cut off the tip of the handle. Either glue the handle to one or both holes or fit it tightly without glue.

RATTLES

Then glue a painting of a turtle, cut out of strong brown paper or stiff cloth, to the box so the ends and sides overlap and may be glued. The handle may also be decorated to complete the work.

Some tribes made fine rattles from gaily painted and decorated dried gourds with wooden handles attached. Effective rattles can also be made from tin cans of various sizes, such as 1-pound coffee tins. Push a smooth, round stick up through a hole in the foot and one in the lid of the can to serve as a handle. Paint the can a bright solid color, with designs painted on it, or cover it with bright cloth and paint designs on that.

Some practice is needed before the brave playing the rattle can produce the rhythmic effects needed to accompany a drum well.

TOM-TOMS AND DRUMS

These are easily made instruments which may be used to keep time with rattles or used by themselves to accompany American Indian songs, dances and stories. The simplest form of drum is made by cutting one end from a

big tin can, such as a cake or cookie tin, using a safe can opener. Any jagged edges left should be smoothed with a file or hammered down. The end is then covered tightly with rawhide, calfskin, chamois or other leather, real or imitation. These can be bought in most hobby supply stores.

The leather drumhead is first soaked in water, then held securely in place by a strong piece of cord or string, using a clove hitch so that the drum cover will not slip. To drop the loops of a ready-made clove hitch over the top of the drum, hold one end of the cord in the left hand and form an *under*hand loop as in A of step 1. Then form an *over*hand loop, as in B of step 1, right next to it. Place loop B on top of loop A as in step 2; then drop the loops over the top of the drum. Pull taut. Finish with an ordinary knot.

A bright design may be painted on the head. For an effective job, the drum may be painted in any color before the drumhead is tied in place. The Indians used chiefly red and blue on their drums, with yellow usually chosen for marking the designs. When a circle of hide is used as a drumhead, it should be painted with watercolors, well rubbed in, after the soaked drumhead has been tied onto the drum.

Serviceable drums can also be made from empty cheese boxes of various sizes, empty nail kegs or old wooden

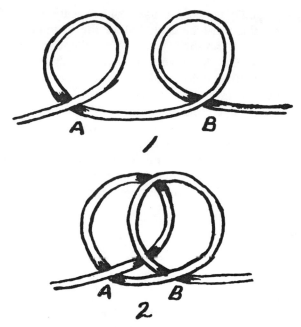

STEPS IN TYING A CLOVE HITCH

chopping bowls. Two-headed drums can be made simply by removing both ends from the keg or box and covering both ends of the drum.

A hole may be punched through the center of the side of the box used to make the drum and a piece of strong cord or leather thong may be threaded through to form a

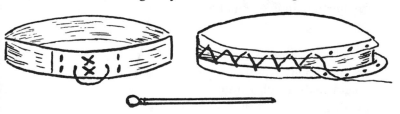

USING A CHEESE BOX FRAMEWORK TO MAKE A DRUM

carrying handle or holder used while beating the drum. Of course, this must be done before the drumhead is tied in place. For a finished look, cover the cord tying the skin head to the drum with a 1- or 2-inch-wide strip of red, blue, or other colored cloth, glued over the cord onto the frame. On large drums, a wide strip about 12 or 15 inches wide, depending on the size of the drum, may be used. This cloth, known as a skirt, is an added decoration on the drum. An easy way to fasten the leather head onto the drum, when this decorative strip is used, is to tack it on all around the wooden frame with small thumb tacks which have fairly large decorative heads.

DANCE DRUM

A number of tribes made huge drums, both square and round, and water drums, but these are too large to copy for modern Indian requirements.

BEATERS

Once the drum is made, a suitable beater or beaters may be fashioned. A serviceable one may be made from a length of 3/8-inch dowel from 12 to 18 inches long, depending on the size of drum it is designed to beat. A narrow strip of cloth is tightly wrapped several times around one end of the stick, tied firmly in place, then covered with a short piece of leather which is fastened securely in place with a thin, strong piece of cord. The beater may be made with a round or pear-shaped beater end.

carrying and storage containers

The Indians employed great skill in decorating their carrying and storage containers. Here's how they did it with medicine bags, parfleches and storage boxes.

MEDICINE BAGS

Useful and decorative medicine bags were made by the Indians for carrying important things, since pockets were not a part of Indian clothing.

The Indian believed that certain things which he found—small stones, strangely colored or shaped, the feather from a bird, a piece of colored cloth, a bead, a shell, a small piece of fur, an oddly shaped root, an attractive weed such as a stalk of fireweed, a piece of buckskin, a bear's claw, and other things—were "good medicine" which brought him good luck. He regarded such things as secret and did not share such secrets even with hunting companions. When we consider that modern people carry charms of different sorts and hang charms in their cars to prevent accidents, this Indian belief appears quite modern. You, of course, can carry whatever you like in your medicine bag, if you make one.

Today, it is best to make a medicine bag from leather or thin canvas, either of which is more durable than felt. Making this bag gives a brave a chance to use the authentic, colorful designs of the tribal group to which he belongs, such as Plains, Woodland, Southwest, or Northwest. These designs may be cut from colored felts and appliquéd, or they may be painted or beaded. A fringe of leather or

colored cloth about 4 inches long may decorate the foot of the bag. The top of this fringe is sewn between the two halves at the foot of the bag so the loose fringe hangs down. The bag illustrated is made in two parts, the easiest way to make it. The two pieces may either be sewn together with strong waxed or nylon thread, or laced together with sinew or other lacing. The bag will last longer and there is less chance of losing articles from it when it is sewn together instead of laced. A strong leather thong threaded through a few small holes near the top of the bag serves as a drawstring and carrying thong.

PARFLECHES

The Indians of the Plains used fold-over leather cases, called parfleches, in which to carry their blankets and other belongings. These were decorated with beautiful designs. Today, boys can make the same sort of case, in which to keep an extra blanket at the foot of their beds, and for personal gear.

To make a parfleche, it is best to draw a pattern first, following the illustration. A parfleche should be made from leather, canvas or strong cloth and tied with leather thongs or tie tapes. The overall length should be about 48 inches and the width about 28 to 30 inches, depending on the size of the leather or canvas used. Paint the outside the desired color—white, cream or buff—and dry it thoroughly. Then fold the parfleche along the dotted lines and draw, then paint a design on the two ends. The back is usually not decorated. Red, yellow, green and black are suitable colors to use.

The parfleche is laced in this way: Pass a short length of thong or tape through the holes at point 1 and tie it on the inside to form a loop outside. Repeat this at point 2.

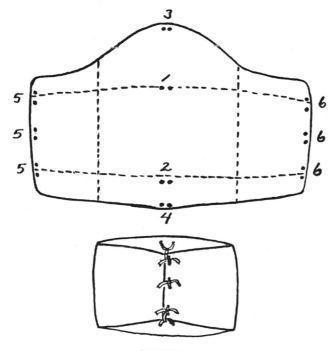

PARFLECHE
TOP: before folding. BOTTOM: folded and laced.

Fold the parfleche along the dotted lines so that points 3 and 4 overlap; then tie them together with a short thong or tape. Now, bring points 5 and 6 together so they overlap about an inch on each side and tie the center 5 and 6 together. Pass the thong or tape of the lowest point 6 through the lower loop before tying the lowest 5 and 6 together. Then pass the thong or tape of the topmost point 6 through the upper loop before tying the topmost points 5 and 6 together.

STORAGE BOXES

Storage boxes were much used and prized by the Indians of the Northwest Coast. They ranged from big to small, were usually oblong or square, and were made from the beautiful red cedar trees which grew and flourished in their coastal habitat. These boxes were decorated with many kinds of colorful designs, either painted directly onto the wood or onto hide with which the box had been covered. The paintings covered tops, sides and ends of these storage boxes.

A storage box can be made from a lightweight wooden box, measuring about 24 inches in length by 14 inches in width and 10 or 12 inches in height. The box can be any size desired. If there is no lid, it is easy to make one.

INDIAN STORAGE BOX

A strip of thin, tough leather about 3 inches wide and the length of the box makes a practical hinge. This leather is doubled and nailed securely to the lid and top of the box with flat-headed nails. When the box has been sandpapered quite smooth, it may be given a coat of paint in flat buff or some other color. When the paint is dry, the desired decorative designs may be drawn on the box and then painted with bright colors. To make an even finer box, the entire outside may be covered with heavy cloth or canvas, then the base coat painted on and the designs added.

chapter
FOUR

Holding An Audience Spellbound

THE AMERICAN INDIANS had many skills apart from handicrafts. Most red men were not only artistic but also had fine inquiring minds which they used cleverly to acquire mental skills. If they had problems which they could not personally solve, they talked them over with the wise men of their tribes. By using their high-powered imaginations, meditating a good deal, and learning from the wise ones, they added wisdom to their skills. This they gladly shared with the younger men and boys of their tribes. The Indian boys also had fine instructors who taught them the outdoor skills dealt with in Chapters 5 and 6 of this book. For instance, men and boys who wanted to become fine athletes practiced hard in hidden places, competed with their friends and in band and tribal sports, and prayed for dream power to show them the way to get the strength and endurance to become fit and strong.

storytelling

To tell a story well, so that the characters in it become interesting and alive, is a great art. Some boys are able to tell a story from memory very well. Others have the ability to make up a story by weaving it out of their imaginations. Either way of telling a story is fine, but to invent stories really well is a great gift, whether they are told to a few boys or at a camp or council fire.

Reading a story, even a very good one, to a few friends or a larger group, is never as satisfactory as telling one. One story well told is worth a dozen good stories well read. For that reason, try to invent interesting tales and try them out on a few friends. Why not trade stories on a turnabout basis, so each storyteller has a chance to tell a story of a certain length? This practice becomes doubly valuable when friends are asked to give frank opinions about the worth of each story and, of even more importance, the way in which the yarn is told.

A good storyteller has the power to make even a poor

story sound good, but when he finds or invents a really fine story, he holds everybody's interest and shines. Really worthwhile stories which thrill by their scope, suspense and action fire the imagination of the listeners and help to make a campfire or council fire memorable.

HOW TO TELL A STORY

A storyteller must be in good form and feel relaxed in order to tell a story well. The audience can soon tell whether one feels at ease, knows what he is talking about, and has something worthwhile to say. A yarn-spinner fares best by sticking to the sort of story he likes most or speaking on subjects about which he has a good knowledge. To be a good teller of tales, one must learn to have the framework of each story set up in his mind's eye, sense when to stress and embroider a point which the audience is enjoying, and touch briefly on a part of the story which has the least appeal.

Telling a good story is the same as writing a good story— it must have three distinct parts: a beginning, a middle and an end. Once the story is begun, there should be no turning back to elaborate and no branching off onto side trails, which may turn out to be dead ends. When the story stops, everyone should feel that it has reached a satisfactory end. The best story loses audience appeal if the narrator allows the story pattern to become blurred. When the framework is clear and sharp, there is no need for explanations which make the story drag. Repetition, rightly and lightly used, can help a story and point up a situation which is about to fit into the tale, but it is most appreciated by very young audiences.

STORY PATTERNS AND ATMOSPHERE

A good storyteller weaves his story like a pleasing pattern. Different sorts of stories require different patterns. To be good, a story must have atmosphere. The right kinds of words in the right places are one means of getting this effect. This is true about Indian tales and stories of the sea and forest; the words in the pattern must be the sort the Indians would have used. The effect of an Indian story would be entirely spoiled if the storyteller used modern slang or modern terms such as: "Gee, that fellow moved! He was out of sight in no time flat." If the narrator uses phrases such as "cat-quick," or "lightning fast," and says that the Indian "seemed to melt into the forest," or "appeared to be swallowed up by the forest," or "merged with the rock," the story does not lose the "feel" of the red man and the forest.

For dramatic effect, off-stage noises can also be used to help a story along in fine style. The distinct snap of a twig, a bird or animal call, the whoop of an Indian, or a "shot" in the mysterious dark which surrounds the council fire circle, all add greatly to the impact of the story being told.

Usually, fast-moving stories should take from five to fifteen minutes to relate. In the case of an experienced storyteller who can hold his audience spellbound, the time may be increased by ten or fifteen minutes.

STORY FRAMEWORK

Indian stories and legends of the distant past usually had a framework that is still used today and was used in many European folktales. In a story of hunting, for instance, it was often the poorest or the least bright of the hunters who succeeded in bringing down the biggest bear or deer. Good luck often favored the least likely character and mishaps sometimes troubled the leading characters in stories of hunting or war.

A story can always be built around a boastful young brave who delights in winning races, wrestling matches, and other feats of strength and skill. He finally meets a spirit, disguised as a poorly dressed, rather small boy, who challenges the boastful one to various tests of strength and agility. It is not necessary to tell who was defeated in each of these events. The punishment of the boastful one is different in each region where the tale is told. As a forfeit, in the Northwest Coast story, he is changed into a Pacific Coast salmon, doomed to the final quest of fighting the many different rapids on an upstream battle which ends in his death. In Plains and Woodland stories, he is changed into a bird, animal, or perhaps a tree.

A story, told among the Northwest Coast tribes, tells of a war canoe with a party of six Nootka who set out to capture a big Haida canoe with only four paddlers. The four Haida paddle desperately to escape but slowly, surely and suspensefully, the Nootka braves overtake the Haida craft. That proves to be their bad luck, because ten more Haida are hidden in the foot of the canoe, and the Nootka are taken prisoners after a short fight.

The Indians were also very fond of stories of animals and birds, magic, mystery and fun, so the modern story-teller has many sources from which to choose as he stands before his brother warriors in the council story-fire circle.

Indian speech ways

Oratory, the art of eloquent public speaking, was just as much appreciated by Indian audiences as it is by the public of today. Nowadays, many public speakers, despite much experience, lose most of the effect of what they are saying by using frequent "ah's," "uh's" and other meaningless monosyllables in order to gain time while trying to think of suitable words. Listening to such speakers is so boring that even if the subject is interesting, the speech falls flat.

Boys do not need to be orators, but by learning the art

of expressing their thoughts clearly, fluently and aloud, they will gain a valuable skill. To be able to combine quick thought with lucid speaking—which means finding the right words as well—and to be able to talk on many subjects on the spur of the moment, can be worth hundreds of dollars.

One way to develop this useful art, even when alone, is to choose a subject at random, preferably one of interest to both the speaker and an audience, and speak steadily for three minutes on that topic. Unless one has a natural gift for this sort of thing, he will find that three minutes a very long time. When a modern Indian has worked up a good vocabulary and self-confidence, he should try speaking for five minutes, then longer, in order to get a good start in the field of fluent and convincing speaking.

The next step is to speak before a small group of friends, asking them to select the subject and, after the talk, to criticize the way the speaker handled it. Speakers should take turns at giving talks so that all may have a chance to see how good or bad they are. They will be surprised to see what practice can do for them.

Indian orators spoke well, in some cases, because they had a natural gift for speaking to an audience—not always a friendly one. Other good speakers won the attention and respect of their audiences because they spoke without fear on subjects about which they felt deeply. Indian chiefs and orators were fortunate because of the many suitable, beautiful words and phrases which they were able to build into their talks. These references and comparisons were made in simple language which their audiences were easily able to understand.

PICTURESQUE SPEECH

Here are a few descriptive Indian phrases, translated into English, which illustrate the beauty of the Indian speech:

- The painted leaves danced with the North Wind.
- The Moon of Painted Leaves.
- The leaves whispered to the stars.
- As many as the leaves on the trees.
- Soon the keen knives of winter will cut the air.
- Fifteen snows. (Fifteen years.)
- Two suns and two sleeps. (Two days and two nights.)
- Many moons. (Many months.)
- So long ago that the time cannot be counted by suns and moons.
- When the moon is round. (At full moon.)
- When the sun looks over the edge of the earth.
- The sun journeys over the edge of the world.
- When the sun is halfway on its journey.
- Before the sun leaves to let the night come.
- When the sun has gone to make place for the moon.
- Farther than a fast pony could run from moon to moon.
- The forest was covered with the dark blanket of night.
- As long as grass grows and water runs.
- The big water was covered with a blanket of sky-colors.
- The water-that-never-freezes. (Ocean.)
- The Star-that-does-not-move. (North Star.)
- The tree-that-whispers-to-itself. (Aspen.)
- The One who guides the wings-of-the-air.
- I have only good things about you in my heart.

When a brave is called on to make a speech at a council fire, he will do best by using simple, picturesque English phrases, using some Indian construction. A little imagination and the displacement of a few verbs in the right places add to the effectiveness and interest of council fire talks and stories. No jargon should be introduced when trying to use Indian talk, since it sounds rather silly to the braves in council who are trying to understand it.

WHAT THE INDIANS CALLED THE MONTHS

It is not surprising that a race which used such picturesque speech found poetic, dramatic, and suitable names for the months of the year. The terms differed widely among the many tribes, though quite a few of them, by chance or through tribal relationship, were the same.

The list of moons which follows gives the terms used by Blackfoot tribes:

January	The Snow Moon *or* The Middle Winter Moon
February	The Hunger Moon *or* The Moon of Wolves
March	The Moon When Waterfowl Come
April	The Moon When Grass Starts
May	The Moon When Trees Leaf
June	The Thunderbird Moon
July	The Moon of Ripe Berries
August	The Hot Sun Moon
September	The Leaves Will Fall Moon
October	The Leaves Have Fallen Moon
November	The Good Robes Moon
December	The Moon When Winter Has Arrived

The picturesque terms which follow were used by various tribes. Sometimes the same name was used by several tribes. Because of this, the tribal origins of the names are not listed. When months are not shown, there were no special names given to these months.

March	The Awakening Moon *or* The Moon of the Crow
April	The Wild Goose Moon *or* The Green Grass Moon

May	The Song Moon *or* The Planting Moon *or* The Moon of Shedding Ponies
June	The Moon of Roses
July	The Thunder Moon
August	The Red Moon *or* The Green Corn Moon
September	The Hunting Moon
October	The Moon of Falling Leaves
November	The Moon When Ice Forms *or* The Moon of Madness
December	The Long Night Moon

Various tribes had equally descriptive names for stars and various natural wonders:

- The Milky Way was known as "The Trail of the Wolf" by the Crow and other Plains tribes.
- The Northern Lights was called "The Marching Lights" by the Sioux nation, and "The Ghost Dance of the Spirits" by the Chippewa.
- The North Star was named "the Star-that-does-not-move," and the Big Dipper was called "The Seven Stars."
- The Iroquois named the sky "The Great Blue Wigwam," and fox fire was called "Witch Lights."

GREAT INDIAN ORATORS

A few of the many fine Indian speakers, who fought with words first, were:

- Chief Joseph Brant of the Mohawk nation of the great Iroquois Confederacy. *Thayendanega* was Brant's Indian name. He was famous in the New York region.
- Osceola, a Seminole chief, an able leader in war and peace. Combating his swamp warfare in Florida cost the United States over $20,000,000, which was a huge amount

of money in the 1830's. The government could not defeat him by strategy, so it was decided to end his successes by treachery. General Jessup of the United States Army persuaded Osceola to attend a conference under the protection of a flag of truce. The chief was then seized and thrown into prison, where he died of heartbreak.

- Pontiac, an Ottawa chief of the Great Lakes region. By the autumn of 1763, this brilliant orator and warrior had built a confederacy so powerful and unbeatable that it shook the British Empire, all-powerful in Canada at the time, following the defeat of the French.

- Red Jacket, a Seneca chief of the Iroquois Confederacy. He was given his name because he received a red tunic from a British officer. He gained no fame as a warrior but much as an orator. He used clever words as his weapon and easily defeated his opponents in the New York region by his skill in oratory and debating.

- Tecumseh, a wise Shawnee chief of the Ohio region. He had great vision and set up a powerful tribal alliance which would be strong enough to allow the frontier tribes to live in peace with the white man. Before the union of the tribes was strong enough to do this, Tecumseh was killed when leading his warriors in battle. Earlier, Tecumseh had told General Harrison, after the Indians had fought for nearly three hundred years to defend their invaded territories, "These lands are ours. No one has a right to drive us from them, because we were the first owners. As to boundaries, The Great Spirit above knows no boundaries, nor will his red children acknowledge any....You and I will have to fight it out."

dramatics and story plays

The Indians combined a gift for dramatics with a good sense of humor, and the result was evident at most of their council and story fires. Fine, exciting stories and legends were dramatized by storytellers at story fires, when dramatic gestures and off-scene stage effects were added to heighten the atmosphere. At times, stories would be enacted in pantomime with a narrator, hidden or standing just outside the council ring, relating in a dramatic manner exactly what was taking place, when the pantomime was not self-explanatory, or the narrator filled in background details and told about what had previously happened. Some of the stories and legends dramatized were sad ones which moved the audience, while other tales were so merry and amusing that even the oldest and wisest chiefs ceased to smile and laughed outright.

Story plays varied greatly and often a serious tale would be acted out, followed by a merry one. Only legends and stories with suitable themes were dramatized. This left those playing the various roles a good deal of scope, which the best actors used to good advantage. Four of the fine legends and stories which can be adapted as story plays are mentioned here.

RAVEN'S REWARD

Raven was a great magician and a trickster too—a legendary figure, half human and half supernatural, known, respected, and mocked by many tribes of American Indians, especially on the Northwest Coast. Perhaps the reason why Raven was so popular was the fact that he often got into trouble caused by his own attempts to be too clever. Even children got the better of Raven at times but sometimes he used his quick wit to get the better of them. One of the story plays, which can be staged in pantomime, tells of the time when Raven, wearing a bearskin, chased some Indian boys from a herring feast which they had spread out ready to eat in front of the fire. A little later, he returned as an Indian, heard about the spoiled feast, and suggested

RAVEN

that some boys return to the village for more fish, especially salmon (Raven was particularly fond of salmon). He told the boys that from that time on they should never be afraid of bears. He said that bears were really cowards and if one should come along to the feast, the thing to do was to drive it off with sticks and clubs.

Raven did not believe that the boys would be brave enough to heed his advice so, after the boys had returned from their village with more fish, he put on his bearskin and, leaving his hiding place, rushed at the boys, growling fiercely as he did so. But the boys had taken Raven's advice seriously and, picking up the thick sticks which they had prepared, beat him so soundly that he was forced to drop his bearskin and show himself as Raven. To his surprise— or perhaps he had guessed it in advance—the boys were so grateful to the magician for having taught them to be brave that they invited him to the feast. As the guest of honor, Raven stuffed himself with fish, especially salmon.

RAVEN AND THE SHADOW PEOPLE

Here is another amusing Haida story about Raven, the Trickster.

This tale can be enacted as a dramatic council fire story

play. Raven, in the play, should be dressed in rather nondescript Indian clothing while the "invisible" Shadow People wear dark blankets, and perhaps masks, and keep out of direct firelight as much as possible. Only two or three Shadow People need perform when the tale is made into a story play, but others may be heard chuckling and making a few strange noises off stage. The play may be embroidered in a number of amusing ways, thought up by the council fire chief in charge of dramatics and storytelling. A brief introduction to this story play may be given by a chief who relates that, once again, the redoubtable trickster, Raven, meets his match, this time in a Haida village without visible inhabitants.

According to the story, Raven was flying slowly over the storm-tossed waters of the Hecate Strait when he saw a Haida village far below. Seeing a chance for possible mischief, and something to eat, he landed on the beach. He took on the form of a man as soon as he alighted close to some other ravens looking for food on the shore. Raven thought himself so clever that he never suspected that keen eyes were watching him from the village. Although he did not know it, he was about to match his wits against the Shadow People.

Raven walked slowly up the wide rocky beach. His tender feet, unused to walking on such a rough surface, became cut by the many mussel shells and bruised by the rocks and stones. He thought for a moment of transforming himself into a raven again, taking wing and landing closer to the village but decided that it was unwise to do so. Someone, he thought, might either see his transformation from human to raven or raven to human. He reached the village and headed toward a large house built of red cedar planks. Voices inside the house whispered, "That trickster, Raven, is coming. Let us guard against his cunning tricks."

Raven entered the huge house and was surprised to see

everything so well arranged. The roof planks had been stacked so that the rays of the sun brightened every corner of the dwelling. He was even more astonished to find nobody in or around the house. There were all sorts of foods stored in the house. Edible roots, barks and berries were neatly piled on shelves, and dried salmon and halibut hung from hooks, ready to be taken down and eaten. This looked like a place where even a magician might be very happy, especially if he were left alone to satisfy his taste for good food, thought Raven.

Though he was not hungry, he decided to have a feast after he had satisfied his constant curiosity by taking a good look at everything in the house. As he moved from place to place, he was startled from time to time by noticing a dark shadow following him. He hurried as fast as his aching feet would let him, then walked so slowly that he hardly moved, but the shadow never left him. He struck downward at it. The black shape did not move, and he heard giggling nearby.

Raven went back to the rack on which the fish hung and took down a big, red salmon. He looked around for a place where he could eat the big fish in comfort. He found a beautifully carved red cedar chest covered with soft sea-otter skins on a raised platform. This was obviously the resting place of a chief. He laid the salmon down beside him while he looked at his injured feet. Then he reached for the fish. It was gone!

Raven had been using his mind a great deal on his transformation work lately, so he could not decide whether he was imagining things or whether he was being deceived by some strange, powerful magic. He went back to the fish rack and took down another fine salmon. This time he laid it within easy reach and decided to keep his eye on it for a moment or two before beginning his feast. He had wondered during the past moon whether his mind was wandering or his willpower lessening. He closed his eyes for a second so that he could concentrate more easily on this matter, which was troubling him greatly. When he opened his eyes, his salmon was gone!

Once more, Raven returned to the rack. Once more he chose a fine salmon. Once more he returned to the seat of the chief to enjoy the fish in comfort. He laid it between his legs and kept his hand on it as he glanced cautiously around. A dark shadow seemed to move on the floor in front of him. With a wild cry of rage Raven took his hand from the fish and jumped and kicked angrily at the shadow. The kicking and jumping had done his weary feet no good, but at least the shadow had disappeared. With a sigh he reached for the salmon. It was no longer there!

Again Raven hobbled to the rack on which the tempting treasures hung. This time he did not unhook a fish because, to his amazement, the three fine salmon which he had so carefully chosen were again hanging on the hooks from which he had taken them.

Raven knew when he was beaten. He limped to the door, with a shadow close behind him, and changed quickly into bird form. He flew swiftly away, leaving the shadow behind. Yes, Raven reflected, his magic was not so strong as he had supposed it to be before his experience in the village of the Shadow People.

LITTLE HERO

Another tale popular at Indian campfires is this one about a little Kwakiutl boy. The boy was very small, but he was also brave and resourceful. The trouble was that the other boys did not know it. He would have liked to play with them but the bigger boys and often the smaller ones would not let him join in their games. Since he had a long name, he can be called "Tsem." One day when the boys drove him away after he had asked to join in a game, he followed them into the forest. He could at least watch them at play.

As Tsem dodged from tree to tree to keep as close to the players as possible without being seen, he saw something which terrified him. "Take care!" he shouted. "The big woman lies behind a great cedar close to you."

"Your words are false," shouted the biggest boy. "You wish to appear big so you may play with us," he taunted as he continued playing.

"I speak the truth," Tsem shrieked. "Beware! Beware!"

Suddenly, the huge man-eating giantess, Tsonerhwaw, sprang forward from the shadows and seized Tsem. She dropped the little boy into a huge basket woven from cedar roots which she carried around her neck. He could not have run away, nor could the other boys, because one glance from the fierce, sunken eyes of the huge witch made it impossible for them to move. One by one, she dropped the shrieking boys into her great basket, shut the lid, hung the basket over her back, and started off toward her hidden home in the deep forest.

Tsem was the only one who tried to think of a way they could escape. The other boys lay huddled together at the foot of the basket, weeping and wailing, while Tsem thought. He tried to climb up the steep side of the basket, but there was no fingerhold between the close-woven cedar roots. There may be another way, he thought. Suddenly an idea came to him. He felt for the little sharp knife which he always carried. Soon, as the giantess forced her way through bushes and underbrush, Tsem started working. It was hard work and he knew that he would have to be quick or they would all be eaten.

Gradually, his little knife blade snicked its way through the tough cedar roots as he slowly cut a hole in the foot of the basket. One by one, the roots parted, and Tsem hoped that the hole would be big enough to drop through

THE BASKET FROM WHICH TSEM ESCAPED

before the wood-witch reached her hidden house. At last the hole was big enough for even the biggest boy to wriggle through. Tsem helped him and told him to see that the smaller boys did not get lost in the forest after the long drop from the foot of the basket.

The big boy trembled as he climbed through the hole. He hung on tightly as he dangled below the basket, too scared to let go. Tsem helped him by rapping him on the knuckles with the handle of his little knife. As soon as the clutching fingers disappeared, Tsem had another boy drop, and one after the other, the boys reached the ground safely. Only Tsem was left, and he got ready to drop.

The huge witch had not heard suspicious noises because of the loud tapping and scraping of branches and the swishing of leaves against her basket as she forced her way through the dense forest. She also did not believe that any of the boys could possibly escape from the basket trap—that is, until the last boy to drop had kicked her hard with both feet as he swung from the foot of the basket before letting go.

With a sigh of relief Tsem dropped straight down from the hole in the basket, only to find himself in the huge hand of the giantess, which she now held directly beneath the hole! The other boys saw from a safe distance what had happened and rushed wildly back to the Kwakiutl village to tell of Tsem's bravery and resourcefulness. "Never again would we have played a game without him," they declared sadly.

"It is too late now," said a chief gravely. "Little Tsem was a braver and better boy than all of you in one skin."

Tsem had made no attempt to struggle out of the huge, fierce fingers which held him so tightly. The giantess brought him close in front of her dim red eyes, which told of her hate and anger. Swiftly, he remembered what he had once heard a wise old shaman say about Tsonerhwaw, the man-eating giantess of the forest. As Tsem was slowly lowered closer and closer to the cavernous mouth of the witch, his forefinger moved in circles in front of her eyes. As he pressed both of his hard, bare feet against the lower lip of the giantess, to delay being swallowed, the words of the wise medicine man proved to be true. The short-sighted eyes of the witch blinked before Tsem's circling forefinger. The eyes closed, opened, and at last shut tightly, for she was fast asleep. Tsem jumped clear as her great body sank to the ground. She still slept as the little boy set out for the distant village.

From the day of his safe return home, the name of Tsem was the first to be called whenever the boys of the village played games.

THE FOOLISH NEPHEW AND HIS UNCLE

Legends which told of clumsy people getting into self-made difficulties, or foolish people, some of them perhaps brighter than they appeared to be, always made popular story plays at story fires. Here is one of that sort.

To make the acting of stories such as this more easily understood by the younger braves in the council fire audience, short dialogue may be used wherever helpful. The audience is soon made to realize that an old man is trying to teach his not very bright nephew to do various things, such as shoot with a bow and arrow, stalk a deer or grizzly bear, or build a canoe. Of course, the young man does everything wrong, in pantomime, and in as funny a way as possible. He shoots his uncle behind the shoulder blade after being told to shoot the grizzly bear there, and ends his canoe-building by driving his ax through the birch bark canoe bottom, after the canoe has finally been built with difficulty.

dancing like indians

The Indian danced with his mind and his muscles. He danced to show what he thought and felt. Much of the dancing done by modern council fire Indians is not spontaneous, free, and natural, because even though the dancers have learned the steps, too many have not entered into the Indian spirit of the dances performed. Of course, the Indian spirit of dance was varied. It could be gay, stately and grave, unrestrained or whirlwind-like. Once a modern Indian dancer has achieved some understanding, real enthusiasm and a good sense of rhythm, the other dance skills will come on fast feet.

To see unskillful Indian imitators prancing around without either pattern or rhythm, wearing ragtag "dance costumes," part Woodland and the rest Plains or Pueblo, is a sad sight. The first thing a participant in an Indian dance should do is to wear an authentic costume of the tribe which he is representing. To add to the knowledge found in books, he should visit a museum which has a section devoted to Indian lore.

WHY INDIANS DANCED

The Indians danced many different dances for many different reasons. Some dances were performed solely for the gods in thanks for some favor granted. Rarely did an Indian interpret such a dance, even for a tribal brother.

The gods understood, the dancer hoped, so what the steps meant was not of importance to anybody else. Indians also danced to assure good hunting, to bring rain, to make the harvest plentiful, to imitate animals and their movements, to be victorious in battle, and for fun.

INDIAN DANCE STEPS

Before any modern Indian can enter into the spirit of the Indian dance, he must know some of the basic steps. Just to jump or hop up and down without purpose and with an overpainted face is not enough. A few of the basic steps, the ones often built into Indian dancing, follow.

Balance is one of the necessary skills in dancing. To develop it, keep your feet under your body and take short steps, except for skip steps and leap dances. Dance with the body relaxed, hands half-closed and legs limber, for most steps not raising the feet more than six or seven inches above the ground. For certain dances, and at certain moments in some dances, the Indians used a crouching position, dropping to a full crouch at times for dramatic effect, but the usual dance position was upright. Various angles of arms and legs, and dipping, rolling and shaking the shoulders all have an important part in real Indian dancing. The graceful, descriptive, rhythmic and sometimes abrupt movements of the arms and hands are adapted to suit the nature of the dance and its mood.

The translated names of most of the dance steps tell how the steps are danced, usually to the tempo of one or more drums.

- *March Steps:* done in an upright position at various tempos, depending on the requirements of the dance being done. Usually done in a straight, forward-march manner, they can also be carried out on place or when moving diagonally.
- *Trot Steps:* a number of short, jogging steps, done in

various tempos on the balls of the feet. They may be done in any direction or on place.

- *Leap Steps:* used in various animal dances, when imitating caribou, deer or elk, for instance. These leaps are made with one foot at a time, and the steps may be in any direction—forward, backward, sideways or straight up.

- *Jump Steps:* made upward, in any direction, with both feet held together.

- *Hop Steps:* done on one foot at a time, as either single or double hops. A hop step is made on the ball of the foot, with the knee of the other leg raised to about waist level.

- *Flat-Foot Steps:* made with the foot lifted in a completely flat position and put down in the same way. The body, from the waist up, is held straight and motionless.

The following are some of the most used dance steps of the Indians:

- *Toe-Heel Steps:* walking steps, taking short steps with the toes placed on the ground first and the heel being snapped down immediately when the toes touch the ground. This step is done in a slightly sitting position, with the back held straight. It is sometimes combined with the pony step (see below) by crossing one foot over the other as the dancer advances.

- *Swagger and Pony Steps:* listed together because they can both be done in a jaunty, swingy way and danced in a wavy pattern. The Indians, especially the younger ones, used a swaggering gait when performing a special dance to illustrate their exploits. The pony step was generally used for moving in a circle or for turning around. It consists of swinging one foot over the other in a fast or slow-moving march step while moving in any direction. When the dancer can perform this simple form of step easily, he may advance to the toe-heel step while crossing his feet.

Sometimes, because of his mood or just for fun, a dancer

would do the pony-twine step, turning round and round on place in such a way that the onlookers got the feeling that the dancer could not stop. Sometimes, to heighten the spectators' belief, a chief or dancing brave would help the "entwined" dancer get himself straightened out.

- *Drag Steps:* frequently used in Indian dancing, these steps can be used for both forward and backward movements. The dancer steps forward on the toes of one foot, snaps the heel of that foot down on the ground, then drags his other foot forward to a position alongside it. These drag steps, also called scrape steps, are also done backward, when the dancer steps backward on one foot, dragging the other foot to a position alongside it. This step may also be done to the right or left of the dancer, the foot on that side being lifted and placed in position, the other foot being dragged alongside it. This step may also be done on place, using alternate feet for each drag step.

- *Stamp Beat Steps:* often used by the Indians. It was thrilling to hear all of the dancers' feet strike the ground hard at the same moment. The four-stamp beat step pattern is done in this way: Starting with both feet together, carry the right foot about fifteen inches to the right of the left foot. Stamp the right foot flat-footed on the ground. This is the first beat. Follow it with three lighter beats made by the same foot. Then return the right foot to its original position beside the left foot. The left foot goes into action when the right foot has completed the movement, and the steps continue as before.

- *Solo Dance Steps:* often improvised by the best dancers, though there are regular dance steps which may be used in solo dances of various sorts.

- *Stalking Steps:* done slowly on the toes, with the feet crossing on a side-to-side movement, either toward the left or right side. Forward and backward steps were also short and stealthy.

• *Fear Steps:* usually half-crouch steps, taken with slightly bent knees, forward, sideways and backward. The head was turned in the direction of the step taken, except when moving backward, and at times both hands were extended, palms turned out as though to ward off danger from the direction in which the dancer looked.

GROUP DANCE PATTERNS

The Indians danced mostly within a circle, usually moving clockwise, but for animal mimicry dances, the dancers bounded and leaped back and forth across the dance circle, as though greeting or challenging the other animals. At times, the dancers formed little areas of four or more animals and danced within the areas which they had formed.

When entering or leaving a dance circle, the Indians sometimes used a snake dance formation, the braves gliding one behind the other, with the chief in the lead. At times, the dancers glided around the dance circle in the snake formation, first winding into a tight coil in a counterclockwise manner and unwinding in the clockwise release.

POWWOW DANCE

This dance is a merry dance with all sorts of patterns or no pattern at all. It was danced by the braves of the Plains and Woodland tribes, among others, as a means of letting off steam. The dancers were on their own in this frenzied fun dance. Though the drums were generally played in double time, with each loud beat followed by a soft one, the dancers often got in two or three steps to each drum beat, as they filled the air with their "hi, ya!", "ho, ho!" and "hi, yu!" yippings. At the end of this dance, the dancers usually rushed from the ring together.

chapter FIVE

Learning the Secrets of the Red Scouts

INDIAN BOYS LEARNED to move almost noiselessly not only in order to become good hunters but for an even more important reason: to roam freely in territory where they were likely to meet warriors from a hostile tribe.

how to move like an Indian scout

Boys can learn to move just as quietly today, but it takes time and practice in various kinds of country to become really skillful. To find out right away if you are clever and quiet on your feet or inclined to be clumsy and move noisily, try this simple test, enjoyed by Indian boys.

In smooth ground, try to move quietly toward a friend who is blindfolded and standing about 40 or 50 feet distant. He must not know the direction from which the stalk is to begin. As soon as he calls, "Ready," begin the stalk, approaching slowly and steadily, taking care to move on the toes and/or the balls of the feet, to suit the ground over which you are moving, as silently as possible. A slightly stooping position, taking care of balance, may prove to be the best stalking position. Trying to creep up can cause more noise than using a more upright position.

Seasoned woodsmen frequently put the heel down first when stalking on grassy terrain, but the toes go first on ground strewn with stones, twigs and leaves. The Indians used the toes of their soft-soled moccasins as extra eyes. While the keen eyes of the Indian scout searched distant bushes for signs of a concealed enemy, his toes felt the ground for twigs, stones, or other objects which could make a slight noise and betray his coming. Once a brave who was forced to stalk across open country reached the shelter of bushes or young trees, his hands joined his feet in assuring silent movement. Careful fingers moved leaves or branches slightly to make it easier to look ahead and, when the coast appeared clear, to allow silent passage of his body.

Once a fellow has learned the art of near-silent movement, he has reached the halfway mark in becoming a good stalker.

There are still two important steps to take in order to rival an Indian scout: taking cover and becoming "invisible."

TAKING COVER

Being able to take cover so that the stalker suddenly becomes invisible to the animal or person he is stalking is a fine art. It requires quick thought and silent movement in order to conceal one's self skillfully. Quick thought is needed to decide in a flash on the very best place in which to find cover. The place must be as close as possible to where the stalker is and it must be the hiding place which has the best chance of concealing all or most of him, while still allowing him to see what is going on all around him, as far as possible. He may decide that a rock, log, bush, clump of long grass, or nearby tree offers the best cover close to him.

Taking cover is only half the skill. A good stalker must know how to use his cover to advantage. Even his shadow can betray him! In order to use cover well, remember:

- never to outline yourself against a light background such as the sky.
- never to look over the top of a rock, log or stump, but always around the most favorable side of it, with head close to the ground.
- to keep both head and body close to the ground when moving over the top of low hills or sloping terrain.
- to use ferns and leafy branches to good advantage, by displacing only one or a very few of them at a time for providing a peephole or slit for observing.
- to carefully avoid all quick, jerky movements when lying in cover. An observer who is watching your position quickly notices something which suddenly appears and disappears, such as a hand, a foot or a head. Movements, when necessary, should be so slow and smooth that an observer cannot tell whether he really saw an object or not.

Indians have developed this very special skill to a very high degree. When one reads that Indians on the hunt suddenly "merged with the forest" or that a lone Indian hunter "melted into the woodland," the writer is quite likely describing what he saw and not what he imagined.

To develop such skill, an Indian takes complete advantage of cover—its color, its shape, even its shade. He knows just where the color of his clothes will blend best with the background and takes full advantage of it. Much of his skill comes from the fact that he has studied the protective coloring of nature on the spot. He has watched animals disappear into the sort of cover which best conceals their presence, and he has learned, partly from them, how to do the same. At night, he does not move along hilltops, even when the sky is dark. He avoids being outlined against a lake or river which, by comparison to his dark shadow, is always luminous, and he takes advantage of the background coloring at all times. By choosing his concealment against a background which he looks for in advance, and by avoiding jerky, revealing motions, he can be seen only by the keenest searching eyes. He moves smoothly, yet quickly.

observing wildlife

Blinds of protective colorings can be used to observe animals and birds without alarming them. A brave can use a ground sheet or light blanket camouflaged by patches of varied, protective, blending colors to cover himself when on an observation hunt. The use of grasses or ferns tied around the head with a dark headband proves helpful at times, but the overuse of such camouflage can be revealing rather than concealing. Difference in clothing color between the stalker and his background is a sure giveaway of his position.

Indian hunters and scouts, dressed for plains or forest,

wore soft, dark clothing, free from bone buckles or buttons, so that their clothing did not brush noisily against trees or bushes or scrape against rocks. Modern scouts have to be even more careful that no bright buttons betray their positions.

Soft-soled moccasins can be worn comfortably by hard-soled feet, but a modern boy may stalk in sneakers or supple leather shoes with thin, pliant soles.

"FREEZING"

"Freezing" is the woodsman term for suddenly standing perfectly still. It is really part of the art of achieving "invisibility." It is the oldest proven ruse for disappearing right in front of an animal's eyes. One may not get the chance to try this trick when he is too close to a black bear for certain safety (and these animals are short-sighted, anyway), but a boy may often get a chance to try this trick when his dog is frantically searching for him in wooded country until he picks up the scent-trail, or when a brave wants a squirrel to come closer.

One of the surest ways of seeing without being seen is to take up a favorable position early in the morning or fairly late in the afternoon. Settle down behind a log or in a brush pile with a hollow in the center so that your arms and legs will not come in contact with branches, leaves or brush which will crackle with even a slight movement. The success of this observation tactic is due to the fact that you are in ambush before the birds and animals come into that area. Even if some are scared out of that section while you are taking cover, most animals are forgetful and will return soon after you have taken up a restful, well-concealed observation post.

Observing animals from a height—whether from a safe crotch of a tree, the side of a cliff, or the platform of a water tower in a camp—also works well. Even easily scared deer will pass beneath the branches of a tree in which an observer is perched. Like some other animals, they look upward far less than they look all around.

WHERE TO FIND WILDLIFE

Of course, to observe wildlife most easily, one must find out first where the animals and birds are most likely to be found and most often to be seen. For instance, the fringes of fields, woodlots, forests and woodlands are far more likely places to find birds and small animals than deep in the woods. Small animals such as rabbits, ground squirrels and chipmunks, and birds such as quail, partridges and pheasants are often seen moving in and out of brush piles and rock piles. They will usually remain inside while someone passes nearby, but if one takes up a well-concealed observation post, even fairly close to the brush or rock pile, he will soon see the wildlife in action again.

Little patches of trees, clumps of bushes and scrub, marsh and small ponds found in flat country are hideouts for different sorts of birds and animals. Wildfowl and mammal wildlife may establish dwellings at one end of a big pond or lake and seem to avoid the rest of the water area. Clumps of long grass, ferns and bracken are considered wonderful hiding places by both bird and beast. The light that filters through the fern fronds and grasses is deceptive and makes observation difficult, and the shadows which they make often help to conceal a bedded fawn or a family of quail chicks from their enemies.

The best position for observing wildlife is with the sun behind one. In this position, one can see the natural coloring of the animals being watched instead of observing what might otherwise look like dark shadows.

STALKING ANIMALS

Most of the pointers given earlier in this chapter will prove of great help in trying to approach the wild things quietly and unseen. The skill developed in moving softly and smoothly, and the ability to take instant cover play an important part in providing the chance to get a good, close-up look at birds and animals.

Correct positions help greatly in getting close to the wild things. The near-upright and half-crouching stances are very good when distance or some handy screen of tall bushes or trees lie between the stalker and his quarry. These positions are far less tiresome and permit quicker approach than either creeping or crawling. Crawling is progressing with stomach and chest mostly on the ground, much of the forward movement coming from pushing with the legs and pulling, when possible, with the hands. Creeping is a hard way to cover ground but it is a little less difficult than the crawling position, since the chest and stomach are held just off the ground. Care must be taken to keep the hips low. Most stalkers find either of these positions tiring for distances of more than about 50 yards.

tracking

This is a very difficult craft and one which an Indian boy learned with a good instructor, much practice and plenty of different animal tracks to practice on. The modern boy can read tracks best on fresh snow, once he has learned the sort of tracks left by some of the more common animals such as the cottontail rabbit, squirrel and raccoon.

To get a good start in following a track, it is best to begin at a point where it shows most plainly, such as on a patch of soft sand or the edge of a marsh or stream. Another pointer is to follow tracks with the tracks between the tracker and the sun so that tiny marks and dents, which are otherwise invisible, stand out plainly.

Perseverance is important when trying to follow a track.

Even when it suddenly disappears, which it often does, if the tracker knows or can deduce the direction in which his quarry is traveling, he is likely to pick up the track farther on. Another way to pick up a lost trail on fairly open ground is to travel in a circle centered on the point where the track was last visible, on the chance of picking it up somewhere on the edge of the circling.

making wildlife come to you

An Indian hunter could actually "call" a number of animals and birds not only by imitating their regular calls, such as the crows' rally call, but also by giving coaxing, curiosity-arousing, and challenging calls. In this way he persuaded the animals to come to him by stirring their curiosity or appealing to their desire for companionship or a fight. At certain times elk, deer and moose are "spoiling for a fight" anyway.

Indian hunters called big game such as moose or elk by blowing on bark horns, while other challenging or friendship calls were made by means of lips, throat or hand claps. Expert hunters were able to easily deceive the most cautious animals and decoy them very close to where the caller was hidden.

BIRD CALLS

Quite a number of birds call their own names, and most of the calls are easy ones to imitate. It should be remembered that most of the birds have other whistled notes and near-songs too. Here are some easy-to-recognize bird calls:

- *Bobwhite.* The two-noted whistle of this bird, "bob-white, bob-white," is easy.
- *Killdeer.* The alarm notes are whistled, "kill-dee, kill-dee."
- *Chickadee.* Its best-known call is "chick-a-dee-dee, chick-a-dee-dee."

- *Phoebe.* It softly and sweetly whistles, "phee-be, phee-be."
- *Jay.* It shrilly whistles, "jay! jay!" or "jay! jay! jay!" or, some say, "thief! thief!"

Most bird watchers and nature lovers agree on the sounds of all the above bird calls, but they often differ about many others, which each person hears in a different way.

ATTRACTING ANIMALS

Since it is often difficult to call animals by imitating their calls, it is easier to attract some of them into showing themselves by working on their keen curiosity.

- Squirrels, raccoons, owls and other creatures which live in den trees can often be brought to a den door or window by rapping on the trunk of the tree with a hardwood stick.

- Chipmunks, squirrels, and sometimes rabbits, can be attracted by lightly tapping two pebbles together.
- Beavers and otters will often surface for a look-see when someone taps gently on the gunwale of a canoe with a stick or paddle.
- Making a sucking noise on the back of the hand with the lips will often arouse curiosity among a number of smaller

animals. A clucking noise made with the lips has the same effect. So does blowing on the edge of a wide blade of grass tightly stretched between the thumbs.

Do not attract wild things by feeding them, because when certain seeds and foods are set out for various animals, they become tame and, after a while, they are caught or destroyed by cruel or thoughtless people.

Indian wildlife wisdom

Field, forest, and woodland challenged the imagination of the Indians just as they do ours. Strange things, birds, beasts, plants and trees were waiting to be found, but it needed sharp eyes, keen observation, imagination, judgment and an inquiring mind to find and enjoy these interesting things. The Indians used all of these qualities to full advantage; not only did they see what was going on, but their power of imagination caused them to invent happenings which were not to be seen by the keenest eyes. The Indians passed many interesting and amusing stories and legends on to us as a result.

These fine outdoorsmen really learned about the birds and beasts and snakes not only by watching them but also through trial-and-error methods which we do not have to use today. They learned which animals were really dangerous and why, which snakes bit and poisoned and which did not. Through firsthand investigation, the Indians learned some fascinating things which they put to good use in hunting and in adapting themselves to the ways of the wild. Here are some of the things the Indians learned:

- Skunks should be left strictly alone.
- No striped snake (the garter snake, for instance) throughout the United States and Canada is poisonous.

- It is not wise to sleep with your head downhill.
- The heads of feeding and idling fish point upstream, and otters on the hunt know this.
- Trout should be looked for in patches of foamy water, where fish food is plentiful.
- You should never swim in a swimming hole where fish may be caught.
- Beavers have only scalelike markings, not real scales, on their tails.
- Squirrels watch you from the opposite side of a tree while you try to watch these wary animals from the near side of the tree.
- Gray squirrels drink a lot of water.
- Several species of butterflies, such as the mourning cloak, hibernate and will fly around in a midwinter sun.
- Badgers are the only animals in the United States and Canada which have a white stripe starting at the nose and ending about halfway down the back.
- It is extremely dangerous to reach into a badger hole to pull out a wounded badger, since the animal's strong bite may imprison its captor even after it has died.
- The track of the hind foot of the black bear most resembles the human footprint.

- Grizzly bears are the only bears which can't climb trees with straight trunks.
- Magpies fly only with difficulty in windy weather because their long tails throw them off balance.
- When stalking wildlife, you should not alarm certain birds, such as jays and woodpeckers, because they immediately alarm everything else within range of their penetrating warning calls.
- Poison ivy itch stops when the parts of the skin affected are bathed with very hot water.
- The only black bird with a brown head in the United States and Canada is a male cowbird.
- By watching the birds and beasts, the coming weather can be foretold.
- Old cobwebs woven across an animal hole, den or burrow mean that the den has had no recent occupants.
- Bothersome hornets can be trapped by hanging a skinned fish of some sort over a bowl-shaped container of water. After gorging themselves, the hornets drop into the water and drown.
- Wolverines are by far the meanest animals. The wolverine needlessly kills any other animals he can, whether he is hungry or not, and breaks and fouls everything apparently just for the fun of destroying things. However, the wolverine is the only animal whose fur does not frost when breathed on in freezing weather, and that is why wolverines were hunted by the red men. The Indians used their fur to edge parkas.

chapter
SIX

Becoming
A
Wary
Brave

THERE WERE MANY dangers which faced the Indians
when on the trails away from their villages, especially in

unknown territory. They included possible attack by enemy scouts or a war party, and being lost long enough to starve. Sometimes a lone brave or several would be attacked by bears, especially the savage grizzly bear, or, in the coldest winter months, wolves. Other dangers were posed by floods, fierce storms, swift streams and treacherous ground which had to be crossed.

trailcraft

Many useful, often life-saving, skills are necessary to feel safe and at home in the vast outdoors. Trailcraft includes several of them. This is something that Indian boys learned when they were very young. Sometimes they developed the many crafts of the trail by the trial-and-error method, which was all right if they were not injured or did not run into serious trouble as they learned. But the boys developed far more skill and avoided most of the difficulties when trailcraft was taught to them by skilled instructors. These men were masters of woodcraft who knew not only how to survive under the most difficult conditions but also how to enjoy life on the trail and avoid hardships. They taught the boys a most useful skill in order to stay alive—how to use their eyes to the utmost.

LOOKING OUT FOR ENEMIES

The Indians knew that to be able to spot their enemies first was a great advantage. Once the enemy was seen, small war or raiding parties knew how to avoid him, and they did so skillfully. Then, after scouting to estimate the number of their opponents, larger bands planned an ambush to take the enemy unawares. Indians made good use of high ground, rocks, hills and even trees, under favorable conditions, to spy on and look out for enemies—and also for big game when on the hunt. Dangerous living made the red men supercautious not only when away from their villages but also in their villages. Scouts and guards were always posted around Indian encampments unless the Indians were grouped in such large numbers, on special occasions, that their enemies would carefully avoid the encampment.

Small bands of Indians on the warpath, who faced the greatest danger when the time came for raiding an enemy village either by daylight or at night, had to be constantly on the alert. Broken branches, freshly bent reeds, the slightest wisp of smoke, a sound which could not be identified as a natural one, a flight of birds of any sort, an animal breaking from cover in the distance, and the noise of a stone rolling down a hillside were all warnings to the Indian scout. Even when things appeared to be serene and quiet— too quiet perhaps—the danger of an ambush was often present. On the other hand, when Indians spotted no danger signs and favorable ones such as a *dry* turtle sliding from a log, they knew that neither friend nor foe had been in the immediate area for at least half an hour.

To make it difficult for enemy trackers to follow them, the Indians on dangerous missions left as little trail as possible. They traveled over rocky ground at times, waded up or down shallow streams, avoided soft or marshy ground where one tell-tale moccasin track might reveal the presence of their party, and in other ways kept their whereabouts secret. After dark, except in the coldest weather, not even the smallest fire was lit. If one simply had to be kindled, the driest tinder and wood was used, and the fire was lit deep in the center of a covering screen built in a naturally sheltered position with extra bush screens added. Often such wise precautions meant the difference between life and death for those warriors on the trail.

FINDING THE WAY

Though the trail-wise Indians, by watching the sun and

stars, usually knew the general direction in which they traveled, this was not enough knowledge to guide lone or small bands of Indians through dangerous enemy country. A band of raiding Indians always sent out a few of its best scouts, often known as "wolves" because they sometimes dressed, howled and acted like wolves when scouting in or close to enemy country. These knowing scouts knew just what calls real wolves used in various circumstances and, what was just as important, that listening scouts or guards around the enemy camp also knew the meaning of different wolf howls.

From a hilltop, a favorite position for observation, these scouts saw rivers, lakes and other landmarks which they knew from the information given them by scouts of former raiding parties lay in certain positions which revealed just where the enemy village lay. Scouts who returned safely to the band with information useful to future raiding parties were allowed to count coup (see Chapter 8), sometimes even grand coup if they returned safely to their own village.

The scouts of raiding parties had to be doubly careful because not only did their capture by the enemy mean likely death but also the important fact that scouts of a band of hostiles were in that territory meant the possible discovery of their band. Another trailcraft skill of the scouts was to be able to find the route back to their own encampment, even after dark at times, since the raiding band knew that their enemies would follow close on their heels in order to take revenge for the raid and possible loss of horses. Some Indian scouts and trailsmen left secret signs which they could read on a return trip to their village but which would either pass unnoticed or be impossible for enemy scouts to read.

TRAIL-BLAZING

Usually, the forest or woodland Indians blazed certain

trails throughout sections of their habitats in order to make getting around easier for the members of their tribe, especially when they lived in the same village sites for several years. To mark and blaze trails in their own area, the Indians used rocks and logs, little stone mounds, and small patches of bark stripped from trees. For long-range visibility marking, all of the branches were sometimes cut from a tall lodgepole pine, leaving only a tuft of branches at the top. Such a tree, known as a lop stick, was really a landmark, since it could be seen for miles from almost any direction.

Today, boys can mark trails without injuring live trees in any way. This is best done by tying small streamers of brightly colored cloth to the ends of tree branches which overhang the trail being made. This method is also good for marking a trail which has become so overgrown that it is difficult to follow. When the end is made wet before using, white or yellow chalk can be used to mark circles, squares or diamonds on tree trunks or big rocks, where these "blazes"

TRAIL "BLAZES"

are most visible. They usually show up well when placed four to six feet above ground. Paint markings should never be made on trees or rocks on public or private lands, though such blazes are useful on private property or private campgrounds, when the owner gives permission to use them.

Blazes about 3 inches in diameter—circular, square or of other shapes—may be cut from thin plywood and painted the desired colors. Fix each blaze to a suitable tree with a 1 1/2-inch, thin nail driven through the center of the blaze, or glue it onto the tree with a little pitch pine resin or other sticky substance. These blazes should be used only on private property or private campsites. One kind of blaze on a tree may mark the way to camp, while a second kind indicates the trail away from camp. Such blazes may be made in code by using different colors and shapes, so that only members of a band may know what the blazes mean or where they lead Perhaps they mark the way to a powwow circle, a hideout, or a food cache, but only those who know the meanings of the secret markings can tell which.

emergencies on the trail

Emergencies arrive unexpectedly when one is on the trail, and they should be met promptly and with a cool head. Quick thought and equally speedy action are often life-savers in outdoor emergencies.

FIRE

Danger from a forest fire can best be met by trying to put a nearby river between one's self and the blaze. When there is no river, the safest place is a stretch of barren ground or a rocky hillside where there is little or no flammable growth. Of course, close to civilization there may be a road with traffic where a car may carry one to safety.

FLASH FLOODS

Sudden, swift floods are a serious hazard. They are chiefly dangerous when they race along a narrow valley or over a stretch of low ground. A heavy rain, especially in country where there are streams fed from sources in the hills, can serve as a warning of the possibility of flash floods. In this case, go to high ground, or if there is little time to reach it, climb a steep hillside, a cliff or, as a last choice, a solid tree.

TREACHEROUS GROUND IN SWAMP AND MARSH

Of course, one should be careful to avoid known swamp-land and marshy areas but, occasionally, even quite innocent-appearing ground is treacherous. The dangerous edges of marshy ground, even though the water-covered stretches appear far away, should not be followed too close. Adventuring on swampy terrain is always very dangerous, but it is much more so when a fellow is alone. Then, such country should be strictly avoided. Woodsmen have often saved themselves from swamp and quicksand by throwing themselves backward instantly and rolling to safety on the spot from which they had just stepped. By this action, they broke the suction of the swamp and temporarily freed their legs from its grip. The only position which offers temporary safety to someone trapped on swampy terrain is a horizontal one, with legs and arms spread out, until a long pole or rope used by a rescuer comes easily within reach of an outstretched hand. Alone, one has little hope of escaping from the dangerous grip of a swamp or quicksand.

FALLS AND FOOT TRAPS

Some very bad falls result from slippery surfaces on the trail. Loose sand and rocks are also unsure footing which cause accidents. Fording water by jumping from one rock to another is a triple hazard, even when the stepping stones appear flat and safe. A rock may be partially covered with a thin coating of sand, it may move or roll under the weight of the jumper, it may be wet enough to be terribly slippery, or there may be a slippery growth growing on the rock. Any one of these hazards is enough to cause a bad fall resulting in serious injury. If stepping stones must be used, the jumper should keep the weight of his body directly above his legs as much as possible in order to keep balance and prevent foot skids. Using a strong, light pole 5 to 7 feet long is very helpful when fording a stream in any manner.

When hiking along a wooded, rock-strewn trail, or on a regular trail where half-hidden roots stretch across the path, keep on guard. A severe fall may result from failing to keep a sharp lookout for these traps. Raising the feet helps on some trails. Keeping a safe distance behind any hiker ahead also helps to make tricky parts of a trail more easy to see.

animal dangers

Even on trails which are not far from home, there are animal dangers which can be avoided. One of the chief dangers lies in making friends with what are apparently friendly animals, and this includes stray dogs and cats. In hot weather, especially, a dog which comes close enough to beg for food may bite a hand which tries to pat him. The scratch of a cat, when one tries to lay hands on it, may become infected and cause nasty poisoning.

SQUIRRELS AND CHIPMUNKS

A squirrel or chipmunk being fed from the fingers may, even without trying, draw blood with its sharp teeth. The bite of any woodland or forest animal can cause infection, and it may be deadly when the beast is infected by rabies—and quite a few of them are.

DEER

Even the gentle, friendly yearling deer are among the most dangerous animals which sometimes stray onto the trail. The actions of deer are unpredictable, especially in fall. A swift downward stroke of their razorsharp hooves can seriously injure anyone who gets too close.

BEARS

These "friendly," funny animals are really dangerous

when upset, and the fact that they are nearsighted adds to the danger. This is because when they reach out, often none too gently, for food held in the hand, they cannot measure the distance accurately. This is why a bear will sometimes wound a hand badly, especially if the person feeding the animal tries to withdraw the hand quickly. The smell of blood will immediately start the tamest bear on the warpath. All shades of black bears can climb trees but, fortunately, the most deadly bear of all, the grizzly bear, cannot.

SKUNKS

The odor-defense of this animal is the least dangerous part of its defense tactics. The bite even of young skunks can be deadly, since quite a few are infected by rabies. Usually if you leave them alone, they will leave you alone.

PORCUPINES

These animals should be given a wide berth, especially when a big one is met lumbering noisily down a narrow trail at dusk. Though these animals are inclined to be peaceful,

and are stupid and slow, hiking and camping braves should be careful when a porcupine gets too close. The only thing fast about a porcupine is its swiftly swung tail; the quills which it leaves in the flesh are difficult to remove and cause a lot of pain. It is best to follow the example of bears, lynx, and even wildcats, and give these lumbering animals leeway. Keep paddles and axes out of their reach, because they are very fond of salt. This appetite causes them to gnaw and sometimes eat the grips on axes and paddles.

SNAKES

It is risky to pick up even a non-poisonous snake, unless one knows how to do so safely, since even non-poisonous snakes give a nasty bite. Boys should learn to identify all snakes in their region. There will not likely be many different species, and a poisonous snake is easily identified by its triangular head, the elliptical (catlike) pupils of its eyes, and a pit between the eye and nostril on each side of its head. Poisonous snakes have long fangs, one at each side of the mouth, with which they inject their venom. Venomless snakes have oval heads, round pupils, no pit and a row of small though sharp teeth.

COPPERHEAD

Never hold a non-poisonous snake even fairly close to your face. Snakes advance their heads in a flash when they decide to bite, and most snakebites in the United States, apart from those on feet and legs, are on the face.

harmful plants, flowers and berries

The seed or berry picker should show everything he picks with the idea of eating it to someone who can absolutely identify it as harmless or otherwise. Any unknown berry, no matter how tempting it may look, may either be actually poisonous or one which causes serious stomach trouble. Some outdoorsmen say that white berries are the most likely to be deadly, but all berries of any color should be looked at with equal suspicion until they have been definitely identified.

There are inexpensive books which illustrate and fully describe harmful American plants of all sorts. To "live off the land" safely, check such books. Many plants and wild flowers, even ones such as the buttercup, can cause skin irritation, especially if one touches the face around the eyes after handling such plants.

POISON IVY

Poison ivy can be found almost everywhere in the United States. This three-leaved plant, shown in the drawing, is shiny green in summer and mottled red-orange-gold in fall, and easy to identify. It should be avoided whenever possible. This is not too easy to do, since it grows behind rocks, up poles and trees, and in clumps of bushes, as well as on the ground—in short, practically everywhere.

When one even thinks that he has touched poison ivy, he must not touch his face or any other part of the body. Washing the hands or other affected parts with strong yellow or green soap, or rubbing them with ammonia, generally re-

POISON IVY

moves the effect of touching poison ivy. Clothing should be thoroughly washed with strong laundry soap before being used again. Never believe that you are not poisoned by touching poison ivy or by poison ivy touching your bare skin. This may prove true one year but not the next. Poison ivy is best left strictly alone!

POISON SUMAC

The sumacs are a group of small trees and shrubs. Even the largest trees of this family are usually well under twenty feet in height. Fortunately, the tree species of sumac grow on well-drained soil. This makes them easy to distinguish from the harmful species, which very rarely grows on such land.

Poison sumac is a swamp shrub, nearly always found on swampy terrain. Its leaves, shown in the drawing, are made up of seven to thirteen shiny, green-grayish leaflets. The edges of these leaves turn vivid orange and red in fall. This

POISON SUMAC

poisonous sumac has greenish-white flowers, which develop into small grayish-white, poisonous berries. These fruits may have helped to create the old saying, "Berries white, flee on sight."

It is fortunate that poison sumac is very rarely encountered on hiking terrain or found around camps, since its leaves are even more poisonous to the touch than poison ivy.

POISON OAK

This is a shrubby, western variety of poison ivy which is not common and rarely found in hiking or camping country. The drawings of poison ivy, poison sumac and poison oak will help you to recognize and avoid them.

BECOMING A WARY BRAVE • 119

making night adventures safer

It's wise to be particularly cautious when moving outdoors after nightfall. There are many minor dangers which would not cause trouble in the light of day but which are full of risk after dark. For instance, a trail should always be hiked before dark when possible because roots stick up from the ground and branches stick out from trees or hang down to trap the unwary. Loose stones, rocks, and slippery sections of the trail can cause a bad fall or perhaps a skid down a steep bank or into a rocky stream. Those who are unused to the outdoors should not engage in night adventuring.

Of course, boys today can learn to navigate in darkness, just as the red men learned. Once the principles of night adventuring have been learned, time spent out of doors after dark will prove very interesting. Nothing looks the same, and things smell stronger and sound louder in the world of night. Caution is the watchword for moving safely after dark. The ears, nose, hands and feet should cooperate with the eyes to make night movements safe and purposeful. Here are a few pointers which Indian instructors gave the young braves who were learning to be self-sufficient on the trail after dark.

IMPROVING NIGHT VISION

In dim light, looking a little to one side of an object which one has lost sight of will help to make it stand out more clearly. Practice in this skill will help to develop it greatly.

Eyes often become blurred from staring too long into the darkness. To correct this condition, close the eyes very slowly, keep them shut for a few seconds and then open them as slowly as they were closed. You can also try blinking the eyes half a dozen times after keeping them closed for about twenty silent counts. If the eyes still blur and fail to do their best night work, focus them on visible objects at various ranges until they become normal again.

By cupping the hands so that they form a pair of binoculars, with thumbs touching in front of the nose, a night explorer can focus on a certain area more easily and effectively.

LISTENING AT NIGHT

By keeping the mouth slightly open, one can hear more clearly, especially in the dark.

SMELLS AFTER DARK

A little practice shows that people can detect smells, pleasant and bad, more distinctly in the dark. This has proved useful to those who became lost at night. Some located a farmhouse, especially the barnyard and pigsty area. Others learned where they were by the strong night smell of wild flowers and certain strong smelling plants, while some, who had developed their sense of smell through practice, were able to detect even the smell of water, which helped to locate a pond, river, or lake, as a night breeze carried the odor toward their questing noses.

chapter SEVEN

Developing Muscle and Wit with Indian Games

THE INDIANS HAD a good sense of humor and appreciated fun. Grownups would play one game for an hour in order to play it better. They never seemed to tire of guessing games, which they played with great skill. Though the boys liked all kinds of games because they were fun, the instructors who taught them knew that they developed quickness of hands, feet and eyes—skills which the boys would need, since the way of life of the red men in those days depended on them. No Indian who could not move fast, silently and almost tirelessly was ever "looked at" by the chiefs—that is, from the Indians' realistic viewpoint, he would never amount to anything. The games which follow illustrate some of the ways that Indian boys learned useful things, in addition to having fun, by contest.

ball games

Indian boys had to make balls of various kinds to play the different tribal games and ones which they invented. Some of them made balls quite cleverly out of pieces of thin leather or cloth, stuffed with hair or grass, while others improvised by using pine cones, gourds and various other things which nature provided.

CLOUD BALL

From three to five boys or more compete in this none too easy game of "catch." The only equipment needed is an old blanket or piece of cloth about 6 feet square and a tennis ball or similar ball. By folding it, two boys can manage the cloth, while the other catches, but five boys is a good number. Four boys sit on the ground, one at each corner of the cloth, with their feet stretched out under it, while the fifth becomes the catcher. If there are more boys present, there may be additional catchers. The boys keep the ball in or near the center of the cloth and, by sharply tugging the corners of the cloth at the same time, send the ball flying high into the air. The boys may take turns at calling "Tug!"

so that the ball is centered well before each throw, but even when the ball is centered, it is likely to take off in any direction. The ball flies further when the tossers stand.

This keeps the catcher or catchers busy not only in catching the ball but also in figuring out in which direction it is apt to fly. Care must be taken not to collide with another catcher. The player who gets under the ball first is allowed to make the catch without interference. After six catches or tries, one of the boys on the blanket takes the place of a catcher, who takes over that corner of the blanket.

To vary the game, balls of different sizes may be used, ranging from tennis ball to basketball size. When using smaller balls, it may be ruled that the catches must be made with only one hand.

HOOP TARGET BALL

This is a modern form of an Indian game which used a hoop made from a withe and either a pine cone or a solid leather ball. It not only teaches the players to catch a thrown ball, but also to throw straight. Today, it is easy to get an embroidery hoop about 10 inches in diameter and a soft ball the size of a tennis ball. A short length of string or cord, to suspend the hoop from a branch of a tree or an overhead wire, completes the necessary gear. The hoop is hung in a convenient position about 8 feet above the ground, with about 20 feet of clear space and smooth ground on each side.

A thrower stands at one end of the cleared space and the catcher at the other, each directly in line with and facing the hoop. The thrower tries to throw the ball underhand through the hoop and the catcher tries to catch the ball with one or both hands. He may run forward, backward, or to either side in order to catch the ball. The game may be played by the two players taking turns at throwing and catching the ball, or it may be agreed that one player throw six times before becoming the catcher.

This game can be made easier or more difficult by using a larger or smaller hoop or a larger ball or by increasing the distance from which the ball is thrown. The supreme test for eyes, hands and feet comes when a helper swings the hoop from side to side!

BALL DRIVE

Indian boys used this game as a test for throwing skill and marksmanship. It may be played in different ways, the easiest one being a game in which only two balls are used, one ball about the size of a tennis ball and the other about volleyball size.

A ring about 8 inches in diameter is marked on the ground, or a hoop may be used and the small ball placed in the center of it. A throwing line is marked about 18 feet away, and the players take turns at throwing the larger ball from behind the line, trying to knock the other ball out of the circle. The ball must be thrown in the same way by each player. Points are given for each time the small ball is driven out of the ring.

A second ball of tennis size may be placed in a ring about 12 inches in diameter, with each thrower given two chances to drive out both balls. The same game may be played with a maximum of three balls, placed in a larger circle about 18 inches in diameter. Players may be allowed to continue throwing, so long as a ball is driven from the circle with each shot, or players may take turns.

DOUBLE BALL

Indian boys could usually invent a game from almost any odd gear they found lying around. This was the case with the double balls, used by the women of various tribes to play a very tough game, with goals 400 yards or more apart.

The double balls, or billets which sometimes took the place of the balls, have to be made first. Two ordinary balls, about the size used for tennis, can be joined together with a strong piece of cord or string so that there is 4 inches of cord between the two balls. The stick, with which these balls were thrown for astonishing distances, was about 44 inches long with a slight knob on the throwing end, but a 24- or 30-inch dowel stick 1/2 or 3/4 inch in diameter will do nicely.

The game was played by having two players stand facing each other about 30 feet apart and toss the balls with one hand by placing the stick under the middle of the cord so that they traveled from one boy to the other. In easy games, they tossed the balls fairly gently and at a level that made them easy to catch. This is the way to learn to play this game. Each player should try to catch the cord which connects the balls in such a way that the balls may be returned to the thrower without their touching the ground. The points for this game may be counted by allowing so many points for each clean catch. This game was made harder by increasing the distance between players and by tossing the balls harder.

STAKE DOUBLE BALL

The same equipment is required for this game as for the preceding one, but a stake about 16 inches long and 1 inch in diameter, pointed at one end, is also needed. The stake is driven about 4 or 5 inches into the ground, where it is smooth and flat. The players stand side by side facing the stake, behind a line marked on the ground 20 feet away. They take turns at throwing the double balls by placing the stick under the cord at about its center and propelling the balls forward with one hand so that the cord strikes the stake in such a way that a ball remains on each side of the stake or with the cord wrapped about the stake. The players either take turns at throwing or a player may continue to throw as long as he scores. One ball striking the stake does not score, but if a ball remains on each side of the stake after the string has struck the stake, the thrower scores three points.

If a 6-inch cord is used, the cord may wrap itself around the stake, unless the two balls strike each other and rebound. This cannot be helped, of course, and it adds to the uncertainty of scoring in this game. The distance of each player from the stake can be increased once the players get a little practice in throwing the double balls.

DOUBLE BALL THROWS

This game also uses two balls tied together, as in Double Ball. The same stick used for the other double ball games may be used as the throwing stick. Each player throws the double balls three times. The object of the first throw is to see how far the player can throw the double balls in a straight line. In the second throw, each player throws the balls as high as he can. In the third throw, each player throws the balls as far as he can, but not necessarily in a straight line. The fact that many Indian women could throw the double balls at least 100 yards should encourage modern braves to try for a record.

In making the first and third throws, it is important that the stick have the right position on the cord which joins the double balls, before the stick is brought forcibly forward and the throw made. The balance and timing must be right or the double balls may drop onto the ground before the throw is made. The same procedure should be followed in making the second throw, except that the stick is brought forcibly upward in order to make a really high throw.

All throws are made from behind a starting line. These contests are best decided on the results of two out of three throws.

hoop games

Hoops were used a great deal by the Indians not only in their arts and crafts work but also in a number of popular games. How to make hoops is told under Hoops in Chapter 3.

HOOP STICK

The American Indians played this game with one stick, while nobles of the French king, Louis XIV, played it with two sticks. Indian boys used hoops of different sizes, ranging from 6 to 14 inches in diameter, depending on how well they played the game, and a stout, smooth stick about 16 inches long. Each player had a stick, and a hoop served for two or more players. A piece of 1/2-inch or 3/4-inch dowel stick about 15 inches long will do.

Two players stand opposite each other and about 20 feet apart at the start of the game. The hoop lies on the ground in front of one player. He picks it up on his stick, either throwing it slightly upward toward the other player at once or twirling it around his stick a few times before letting it glide. The other player tries to catch the hoop on his stick and return it to his opponent. It takes practice to do this. The game continues in this way, players losing points each time they fail to catch the hoop.

The game may be made more difficult in several ways: by increasing the distance, by decreasing the size of the hoop used, and by throwing the hoop harder. Several players, standing about 20 feet apart, can keep the hoop flying from one to another without letting it touch the ground.

HOOP TRAP

This game is played with two hoops, one slightly larger than the other. The nearer the two hoops are in size, the more difficult the game. It is always more difficult to play this game with smaller hoops. If the game is played with two fairly large hoops, one measuring about 12 inches and the other about 10 inches in diameter, it will go well. The larger hoop is placed on flat, smooth ground about 15 feet from a throwing line marked on the ground. A boy standing behind this mark tries to glide the smaller hoop inside the larger one so that it remains there instead of bouncing out. A boy may continue to throw until he fails to score. Then his opponent takes the throwing hoop.

An increase in throwing distance makes it more difficult to score, and the nearer the two hoops are in size the harder it is to throw the smaller one inside the larger one. Players may invent methods of scoring, allowing points for a hoop which lands nearly inside the target hoop but with part of it resting on the rim of the bigger hoop, or giving points for the hoop which fails to go inside but lands closest to the target hoop.

ARROWHEAD HOOP THROW

The only gear needed for this game are three hoops 12 inches in diameter, a paper plate, and three large, pointed paper drinking cups, measuring about 3 3/4 inches high and 2 3/4 inches across at the rim.

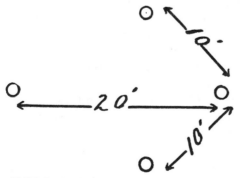

PLAYING AREA FOR ARROWHEAD HOOP THROW
The circle on the left represents a paper plate. The other three circles represent paper drinking cups.

The paper plate is placed on a piece of flat, smooth ground 20 feet away from the center cup, and the three paper cups are spaced 10 feet away from each other in the form of an arrowhead. The contestants stand beside the plate, facing the cups, and try to ring each of the three cups in any order. Each cup ringed counts three points, and a score of eighteen may be counted as a game. Two or more players can contest, one player standing on each side of the plate and taking turns, or each player throwing three or six times in succession.

MAYAN HOOP BALL

This was a very strenuous game which could only be played by the toughest players. It is played nowhere in the world today. The Mayans contested this game between two teams with seven players on each side. The object was to bounce a big, live-rubber ball through an upright metal hoop, only slightly larger than the ball. The hoop was placed 18 feet above ground level. No holds were barred as each team fought to break down the other and break up its defense, each team trying between terrific scrimmages to score the one goal required to win the game. In the circumstances, it is not surprising that it took two or three hours of continuous play to score that one goal, when one considers that the goal could only be scored by bouncing the ball through the hoop from a head, hip, or arm, hands being barred!

The end of the game well illustrated the saying "Winner takes all," because those of the winning team who could still get around rushed into the grandstands (while the spectators rushed out) and helped themselves to anything they wanted. No remaining spectator dared to refuse whatever demand a victorious player made.

An up-to-date version of this game, scaled down for younger players, may be played in this way. Two teams, with four members each, try to drive a soft, bouncy rubber ball about 6 inches in diameter through a stout hoop, 12 or 18 inches in diameter, set upright in the center of a smooth play area, but only 9 feet above ground level. To make this modern version easier, the ball can be bounced through the hoop by a head, shoulder, or fist, with open hands being barred. The players may block their opponents and endeavor to snatch the ball, but must not hit or hold during the game. The winning score may be one to three goals, one point allowed for each goal, and the play may be divided into four 15-minute periods, or a shorter number of periods, should the number of goals decided on be scored earlier in the game.

This game may be made easier to play by setting up two hoops, one at each end of a smooth piece of ground about 70 feet long and 30 feet wide. In order to play this modern version of the game in Mayan fashion, off-sides and all other similar technicalities can be ignored.

races and race games

Indian boys were very fond of racing, since it could be carried out without any equipment and on smooth ground or rugged terrain. The old call of "I'll race you!" was often heard in and out of Indian encampments. Fleet-footed long-distance runners shouted impossible challenges such as "I'll race you to the sunrise" or "I'll race you to the sunset," and many took up the challenge, racing until they dropped. None of the following races have impossible goals, but all of them assure exercise and often amusement for both runners and those who watch.

STRAIGHT RUNS

Indian boys ran straight races to a given mark, racing distances ranging from 50 to 500 yards or more. Sometimes, to arouse greater excitement among the onlookers gathered behind the starting line, the races were of the there-and-back type, the runners returning to the starting point, where the race ended.

RACE AND STOP

This race was used to teach the runners to stop—fast! A line may be drawn to mark the start and another to mark the finish of a 40-yard run. Ten yards from the start, a white strip of cardboard or a paper drinking cup can mark the spot where a full stop must be made in a second or less. Ten yards farther along, another stop point is marked, and the third and last is marked 10 yards from it. These stop points are set out directly opposite the starting point of each runner.

On the word, "Run!", the runners race, each one observing the stop points on the way to the finish line. The contestant who finishes first wins, provided he has made the best, most complete stops.

Such races taught the young braves to stop in a hurry— quite often a life-saving skill when people lived dangerously as the Indians did.

FORWARD-BACKWARD

Several teams of two boys each can compete in this race. Each pair of boys stands back to back on a line marked on the ground, with about 3 feet between teams. Each two boys link arms at the elbow and stand with one boy facing a line marked on the ground about 30 feet away. On the word, "Go!", each team races as fast as possible to the distant line, which the racer facing backward must also cross. Then each team returns as fast as possible to the starting line, the brave who raced backward now leading and facing forward. The starting line becomes the finish line, and the first team to cross it becomes the winner. This makes an amusing race when several teams compete.

FORWARD-SIDEWAYS

Two boys forming a team stand back to back, arms locked

at the elbows as in Forward-Backward, but they stand sideways on the starting line. Another line is marked on the ground about 30 feet away. On the signal, "Go!", they race sideways as fast as possible to the distant line. As soon as the team crosses the line, it starts back to the starting line, which has now become the finish line. The team crossing it first is the winner. This race can be made harder or easier by increasing or reducing the distance to be run.

DOUBLE CROSS

This stunt-race is carried out the same way as Forward-Sideways except that each brave crosses one foot over the other, then brings the rear foot alongside the other, racing sideways to the distant line. This step is repeated as quickly as possible until the line 30 or 40 feet away is reached. For younger boys the race can end here just as soon as the team has crossed the line.

For bigger contestants, the race continues back to the starting line. This means a reversing of foot movement which slows down some racers and quickens the pace of others. These changes add to the fun and uncertainty of the race.

LOOPER LOPE

Indian boys delighted in imitating the movements of all kinds of animals and birds and found pleasure in moving and racing in the different positions in which these creatures moved. In the amusing race given here, the boys copy the movements of a "looper," better known as a measuring worm. Two or more boys race each other. On a smooth piece of level ground, preferably grass, the boys stand side by side with 3 feet between them. They face a line marked on the ground about 30 feet distant. The contestants stoop until the palms of their hands and forearms rest flat on the ground, the tips of their fingers just behind a starting line. The feet and legs are then stretched out straight behind

MEASURING WORM

the body, which is balanced as securely as possible on the tips of the toes and the palms of the hands.

On the word "Lope!", each "racer" short-steps his feet forward, one at a time, until both feet are directly behind his hands. He then advances his hands forward, one at a time, until he is in the starting posture again. These movements are repeated as quickly as possible—and that will not be very quick—until the racer crosses the finish line.

Older and tougher players can continue the race backward to the starting line, carrying out the movements in reverse while trying to move in a *straight* line. Anybody watching these backward loopers trying to hold a straight course is in for fine fun.

This race, in either version, can be run as a relay, with from two to four on each team.

The winners should be judged as the Indians judged them, by their form in advancing and retiring, as much as by their speed. Any looper who advances his feet up to or away from his hands in only one or two motions, instead of by several tiny steps, may be ruled out of the game.

KICK STICK RACES

The kick stick was used originally for highly contested challenge races, run by Indian men and boys of the Woodland, Southwest, and Northwest Coast tribes. The distances covered by the kick stick racers ranged from five to ten miles or more. Some Southwest tribes used these races as part of a ceremony to bring rain for the corn.

The average kick stick was made from a perfectly straight hardwood stick from 2 1/2 to 5 inches long and from 3/4 to 1 1/2 inches in diameter. Most sticks had identifying designs burned into them to show ownership. Kick stick races were contested in two ways. Sometimes each kicker had his own stick and at other times there were two to four players on a team, all of them kicking the same stick. Only the feet could be used; a player who touched the stick with his hand was out of the game. These races were won by whoever kicked his stick over a finish line first.

Today, boys can play this game in either of the above ways. Strangely enough, the runners move fast and do not appear to tire easily. The Zuñi believed that the kicked stick "drew the runner along with it," so long as he kept the stick moving ahead of him. Some tribes believed that there was much "medicine magic" in these sticks, and owners did not part with their favorite sticks.

Some modern Woodland Indian youngsters on a Six Nations reservation showed the author a very amusing version of these kick stick races. Since then he has often demonstrated the game at Indian Days and council fires, where the activity rings were rather large. The Woodland boys were using a kick stick about 10 inches long and about 3/4 to 1 inch thick. The strangest thing about the stick was that it was crescent-shaped, and that is where the fun came in! The Indian boys made the stick from a green, supple stick of the right size, by pulling the two ends towards each other, tying them in that position when they were about 5 inches apart, and letting the stick dry so that it kept its half-moon shape. Some sticks can be steam- or heat-treated into crescent shape so that they keep the curved shape when dry, or a hoop about 6 inches in diameter can be cut in half, making two kick

CRESCENT-SHAPED KICK STICK

sticks. Kick sticks may be decorated with paint stripes or in other ways by their owners.

Amusing races can be carried out with these sticks on fairly smooth ground or around a council ring. Even then the kickers are very careful, as these crescent-shaped sticks are liable to fly in any direction except the expected one.

guessing games

Indians were fond of guessing games, most of which were quite simple except for the fact that it was hard to guess right. They required no equipment except some pebbles, a piece of rope, a few sticks and the like.

ONE, TWO, THREE?

Two players sit facing each other about 6 feet apart. One player holds three small pebbles behind his back. (Small marbles can be used instead.) When the pebble-holder decides how many pebbles he will use, he brings a clenched hand from behind his back with one to three pebbles in it. The guesser touches or points to the hand and states the number of pebbles which he thinks it holds. The hand is instantly opened to show whether the guesser is right or wrong. If the guesser is right, he does the pebble hiding, but if the guess is wrong, the opponent continues until the guesser is right.

In the old days, the player concealing the pebble sometimes sang snatches of song, usually off-key, to throw the guesser off balance, and modern Indians may do so too.

This game was made twice as hard by using both hands and having the guesser decide not only how many pebbles were hidden but also in which hand, since they could only be concealed in one hand for each guess.

GUESS STICK

This was one of the simplest of the so-called hand games. It was enjoyed by thousands of Indian boys. It was played with two sticks, each about 1 1/2 inches long and about 1/2 inch thick. (Two dowel sticks will serve very well.) One stick had either a thin line burned around its center or a thin painted line to indicate that it was the lucky stick. The players sat facing each other as in the preceding game. One player held the two sticks behind his back and made a series of lightning-fast motions with his hands and arms as a part of his stick-hiding technique. Some of the manipulators of the sticks worked with their hands held out in front of them, but the speed of the changes made it just as hard or harder for the guesser to tell in which hand the lucky stick ended up. Sometimes a stick holder held one hand out with a smile which suggested that the lucky stick was in that hand—and quite often, it was!

stalking games

Indian boys liked stalking games. Some were played as wide-ranging games in the woodland or forest while others were played in much smaller areas.

In the wide-ranging games, a keen-eared, keen-eyed spotter stands in a little clearing among the trees and, with his eyes closed, counts slowly up to forty or fifty. While the spotter is counting, three to twenty stalkers all rush in different directions for cover. At the end of his count, the spotter blows a loud blast on his whistle. The object of the game is for tne stalkers to approach the spotter without being seen or heard. Each stalker uses every bit of cover available to him, to avoid being seen.

It is agreed that the spotter will move in a circle not more than 10 feet in diameter, without leaving the clearing. The spotter searches the forest for signs of movement. As soon as he spots a stalker clearly enough to be able to call his name, he does so and the player returns quietly to the clearing, while the others remain without movement. When the spotter sees some part of a poorly concealed stalker but not enough to identify the player, he calls out the color of clothing he sees and, when possible, describes some prominent object near t'ie stalker, such as a log, rock, or paper birch, which tells the boy who was spotted that it is he. That boy immediately goes to the clearing. In fairness to the spotter, all other stalkers remain where they are until the spotter has stopped calling out the description, or he may blow a single blast on his whistle to let the hidden players know that the stalk may begin again. The braves who approach closest to the spotter are the winners.

Another popular form of stalking may be contested by two players wearing soft-soled moccasins or sneakers. The contestants are placed about 10 feet apart. One is told that he is the deer and the other is the stalker. The stalker is blindfolded, with ears left uncovered so he can hear. When the chief calls "Stalk!", the deer moves off slowly and quietly in any direction, but trying to move more or less in a circle, while the stalker, moving as quietly as he can, tries to follow it at fairly close range but without touching it. The deer doubles in his tracks, "freezes" and uses any other ruses it can think of, in the hope that the stalker will pass him and go astray. After two or three minutes of action, the chief decides whether the deer or the stalker won the contest.

Indian signal

The American Indians employed small mirrors, even ones made from tin lids, very skillfully for signaling. They used these signal mirrors to tell each other about animals which they wanted to hunt, and to warn of an approaching enemy scout or war party. Indian chiefs directed the movements of mounted groups of Indians by the clever use of a mirror.

Today, small mirrors are often used by lost persons to signal a low-flying airplane with their flashes. To use a mirror well, one must be able to focus the rays of the sun quickly and accurately by using the mirror as a lens. Here is a game to test the players' skill.

Two or three boys stand side by side and close to each other. Each tries to shine the light reflected from a small round or square mirror onto the smooth polished lid of a tin can or a small mirror attached about 6 feet above the ground to a tree or pole. To start the game, each boy, with the sun in front of him, stands about 20 feet in front of the target, holding the mirror in one hand behind his back. On the signal, "Focus!", each boy instantly brings his mirror in front of him and tries to shine it directly and steadily on the target mirror. The first boy to focus his mirror directly on the target and hold it there is the winner.

This signal game can be made more difficult by increasing the range and, harder still, trying to focus on the target while standing at an angle. A little practice will soon increase the focus speed and accuracy of the mirror flash.

chapter EIGHT

Staging Coups, Ceremonies and Challenges

TODAY, THE Olympic Games give athletes a cnance to show their form and skill. The American Indian, also had their simple form of these games, in which the young men and boys contested in many Indiancraft skills and showed their strength and know-how in man-to-man challenges. The braves who won the various matches, tried hardest or gave the best performances, were allowed to count coup in honor of their victory.

coups

The words "coup" and "grand coup" are French terms, introduced by the early French adventurers and adopted by the Indians. Though the word "coup" actually meant a physical blow, the general meaning covered not only brave and skillful deeds in hunting and battle but also clever strategies of any sort in practically all ways of life, active or passive.

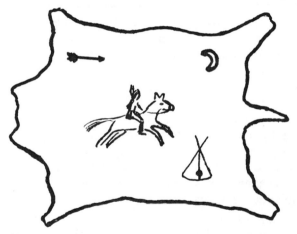

SACRED RECORD OF A BRAVE'S EXPLOITS DRAWN ON BUFFALO HIDE

A grand coup was a bigger and more important achievement than a coup. A brave could gain a feather for a coup, but for a grand coup the feather was decorated in some distinctive way. Some tribes, especially those of the Plains, tied a

COUPS, CEREMONIES AND CHALLENGES • 141

small tuft of horsehair to the tip of the feather. This tuft was usually dyed red. Other tribes cut and notched feathers in different ways to indicate coups. Of course, counting coup for athletic achievement was only a small and less important part of the coup award system. Coups and grand coups were awarded a warrior who struck an armed enemy brave in battle with his hand or who was especially skillful in warfare, hunting or scouting.

CLAIMING COUP

Later, at a council fire, a brave who had performed a deed worthy of earning a coup or grand coup was called by the chief to enter the circle and tell the chiefs and assembled warriors of the deed he had performed for which he wished to count coup. As may be imagined, some braves were modest in their statements. Some even used understatement, but others, carried away by the occasion and the honor of appearing before the chiefs and braves, gave a dramatic, exaggerated and not always exact account of what they had done. In order to keep the coup statements as close to the actual deed as possible, different Indian nations and tribes had special wording to be used as part of their coup declarations. It was a sort of oath which usually forced the brave making the declaration to stick to the facts. The mighty Six Nations of the Iroquois, for instance, had the coup-claiming warrior hold up a string of wampum or a wampum belt at the end of his claim and declare, "This thing did I do and this belt upholds my words."

A Dakota of the powerful Siouan groups declared, "My words are true! Earth hear me and refuse all help if my words are false." Other Siouan groups made their coup claim while calling on the Thunderers, spirit beings who could punish them terribly for speaking with a "forked tongue." Braves of the Blackfoot nation threw a stick on the ground when counting coup. Many prairie tribes swore on a pipe (calumet) when declaring coup, since no Indian dared speak falsely on a pipe. A Comanche brave of the Southwest recited his coup claim while calling on the sun (father) and earth (mother) to confirm his deed. Later, within two circles of chiefs, he claimed coup while shouting at the top of his voice, "I claim coup!" The leading chiefs either granted or refused the coups claimed, and those making the claims accepted the decisions stoically.

COUNTING COUP

When a brave was allowed to count coup, most tribes had different ceremonial ways of doing so. The braves of some tribes counted coup by striking a decorated coup pole, set up in the open or in a big tepee. The pole was struck with a coup stick, tomahawk, stick or club, after the claim had been recited. (How to make a coup pole is told in Chapter 3.) A Crow Indian either pushed a long eagle feather into the ground and repeated his claim statement, or he drove a short pointed stick, decorated with little bunches of "fluffies" (downy "breath feathers") tied to the top, into the ground before his recital. Some tribes used drums during the coup-claiming ceremonies, the thunderous stroke from a big drum being used immediately after the coup claim had been made.

COUP POLE CEREMONY

For this ceremony, an important one in which braves claimed coup feathers for deeds well done, a coup pole (described in Chapter 3) was set up in the council ring in a position which allowed coup claimers to dance around it easily. How the braves claimed coup has been briefly told in the preceding pages. An elaborate coup-claiming ceremony may be built around the statements of the braves, made as they strike the coup pole and claim coups. The chief may question a few of the braves who make claims and the braves reply in a loud clear voice. Usually, no claim is refused at such ceremonies, since each candidate has been questioned beforehand and his claim has been either acknowledged by the examining chiefs and medicine men, or refused, so that no claim is made by him at the council fire.

COUP CLAIM DRAMATICS

Occasionally, among the Indians of times gone by, a coup claim made by a brave was challenged by a chief or another brave at the time that the claim was made in the council ring. This was a dramatic moment, since a claim was challenged unexpectedly, and it sometimes required the power of the chief and the medicine man to keep the braves from settling the dispute on the spot with hunting knives. The one who claimed and the one who refuted the claim, from personal knowledge which he had withheld until that moment, then had to make statements before the assembled braves as to why the coup had been claimed and the right to it challenged. It took a wise chief, perhaps aided by the medicine man and some of his councilors, to openly decide the matter so that neither of the braves was too deeply offended. Occasionally, a decision was withheld for a day or two, both braves being warned to wait patiently, in order to decide the matter fairly.

Such a dramatic moment, planned and carried out, but with only the chiefs and principal actors knowing what is going to take place, can prove most effective at a modern council fire. It can illustrate the boastfulness and foolishness of claiming too much for performing too little. It can show how a brave who hated to carry tales was forced by circumstances to take action. Last of all, and perhaps most important, it demonstrates to the braves in council and all concerned how chiefs, by their reasoning, logic and fairness, became the leading men of the tribe.

The incident which provides the dramatic clash might be based on an old-time claim, such as the claim of having chased, caught and killed a wolf with a hunting knife, or having invaded a hostile camp in disguise, and the like. It can also be adapted to modern circumstances by having a candidate claim that he climbed a high peak alone or swam across a wide river or one with a strong current. The chief in council may then point out the danger and foolishness of such acts. After the council fire, following such dramatics, it is made known that the denied claim was staged purposely to try the acting powers of those taking part and also to give the audience a dramatic experience.

Indian ceremonies

Fine Indian dress and regalia should be used for various ceremonies which are full-dress events, besides council fires. The old-time Indians had many of these ceremonies. Some were celebrated by an entire nation, tribe or band. Others were performed by lone Indians who wore their finest clothing and disappeared into the depth of the forest or climbed high into the mountains to offer thanks or ask the sun, earth, or their own special medicine-magic for help in some very difficult situation which had arisen or which these Indians knew was coming.

SALUTE TO THE SUN

From time to time, various tribes, including the Comanche, saluted the first rays of the sun in various ways. The Comanche had three of their finest warriors, in full regalia, greet the rising sun with three high, quivering wolf howls. This ceremony, usually to give thanks, was often attended by an entire band, wearing their finest dress. These braves stood with their hands and arms uplifted toward the east while the salute was given. Afterward, the leading chief burned a wisp of "sweet grass" before the band so that the fragrant aroma of the burning grass would please the sun to whom they gave thanks. Boys today can work out suitable things to do at such ceremonies which would not have displeased the earlier red men whose traditions they try to uphold.

Ceremonies to honor the setting sun for the good things that have happened during the day, to honor the sky for much-needed rain which has fallen, to honor the wind from the north, south, east, or west for some benefit which it has brought, such as coolness during a very hot period, are a few suggested ceremonies which may be carried out during daytime. An Indian Day may follow these ceremonies, with games, contests and challenges for which the participants change to their old breechclouts until after these events.

COUNCIL FIRE CEREMONIES

There are many after-dark ceremonies, apart from pageantry and storytelling. One of these is the Hiawatha Firelighting Ceremony. In this, a leading chief, with a fan of feathers shaped like the wing of a gull in his hand, stands before the unlit council fire with the medicine man. He stoops and brushes the ground in front of the council fire and throws a few small charred sticks to one side. He tells the assembled braves that he is doing as the great Hiawatha did, brushing aside the ashes of the old fire with the wing of a gull, that the new fire may burn bright at their council that night.

There are a number of impressive calumet ceremonies

CALUMET

used in various Indian tribes for the opening of the council fire. In some, the beautifully decorated pipe is real. In others, it is an imitation one, so that smoking it is done in pantomime. The pipe was either carried ceremoniously, pipe and stem resting on both outstretched hands, to the fire by the leading chief or medicine man, or carried to the fire on the order of the chief by the Keeper of the Pipe. The pipe is then lit by the chief, medicine man, or pipe bearer.

The ceremonies vary greatly from that point on. A chief can blow a puff of smoke or point the stem of the pipe toward the sky, home of the Great Spirit; then the earth, mother and giver of food, is similarly honored. After that, the chief may point his pipe stem to the four cardinal points, from which comes the wind. A number of tribes used this sequence: East, South, West and North. Others carried out the pointing ceremony in this order: West, North, East and South. As the chief points, he gives the reasons why the braves in council, through him, are honoring these points. The earth is honored for giving many good things; the East, that the sun may return when night goes; the South, that its warm breath may bring comfort after the cold of the night; the West, as the sleeping place of the sun; and finally the North, that its sharp wind-knives may not harm when it makes the painted leaves dance and when the earth wears its snow-blanket.

OPENING A MEDICINE BUNDLE

Many an Indian tribe possessed a collection of sacred objects. Such a collection was always guarded by a special keeper and carefully rolled up in a medicine bundle. Opening this bundle, usually on very special occasions, called for an interesting ceremony which is still very effective as part of a council fire program.

These sacred bundles were assembled and regarded with awe and reverence by many powerful tribes, such as the Pawnee, Sioux, Omaha, Osage, Fox and Winnebago. Most

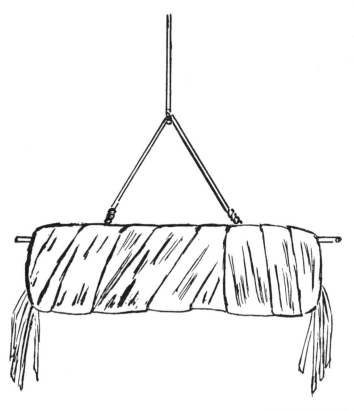

MEDICINE BUNDLE

of these bundles were covered by an oblong piece of buffalo hide, generally with the hair outside, measuring about 4 feet long by 2 1/2 feet wide. When the sacred objects were placed on the hide, it was rolled up into a more or less oblong bundle and securely bound with rawhide thongs. The bundle was decorated at both ends with a fringe of rawhide, or strips of rawhide or red flannel. Each tribe had its own special ceremonies for opening these bundles. Usually two or more braves in full regalia brought in the bundle, often slung from a pole, sometimes painted red, to an accompaniment of drums and rattles, used softly. The bundle bearers stopped beside a big animal hide or colorful blanket, where the medicine man was waiting. He told the assembled tribe that the bundle had been good to them during the past moons and that the braves should sing as he prepared to open the bundle. He did so, and the sacred objects were carefully spread out on the blanket. The bundle was remade with equal care.

challenges

Challenges were often a part of the council ring activities, and for modern council fires, various challenges—man-to-man, band, or tribal—can prove interesting as well as exciting activities. Some challenges were serious contests to test the strength and skill of the contestants, while other challenges were amusing ones which appealed to the sense of humor of the red men.

Sometimes fun challenges were based on serious activities, such as Indian dances and dance plays, and sometimes they were based on stories and legends acted out in a lighter vein. Some tales told by storytellers of the plains and woodlands were funny ones which could be acted out as challenges in amusing ways, such as the one which follows.

As planned, during a council fire a boastful young brave who dances fairly well enters the council fire circle and, after saluting the chief, performs a few brisk dance steps. He then challenges any dancer among the assembled braves to dance better than he does. To everyone's surprise an old man (he can be a young leader or councilor made up as an old man) hobbles into the ring and accepts the challenge. The young dancer may do a difficult dance, either improvised, or a real Indian dance, such as the Dance of the Flame or the difficult Pipe Dance. To his apparent astonishment, the old man outdances him amid the approving "Ho! Ho's" of the braves in council. The young brave admits defeat, states that he will try to become a better dancer and leaves the council ring with an arm around the old dancer's shoulders.

The red men contested many man-to-man challenges. Some were hard work, while others were fun challenges, though they also called for various skills and strength and were amusing to watch. Because of this, many challenges in this category were favorites at council fires which were devoted to storytelling, dancing and challenges.

Though a number of challenges by bands, tribes and individuals may be planned in advance, sometimes an open challenge night in which any brave may challenge another is a lot of fun. One brave stands, salutes the chief, and says something like this: "Is there a brave in this circle who dares to accept my challenge to a back-on-ground wrestle?" (It is best to use simple forms of challenge activity such as the one known today as Indian wrestling, instead of allowing really strenuous athletic events at a challenge fire.) The challenge is usually accepted at once, and it is the job of the leading chief and other chiefs whom he may appoint to see that the two braves who contest any of the man-to-man challenges are fairly evenly matched.

The following are some novel kinds of man-to-man challenges.

THE BACKWARD FROG

This is a twice-around-the-circle council fire challenge which brings laughs from the spectators. Two contestants squat in frog-hop positions facing each other at the center of one end of the council ring. They balance themselves by holding each other's knees. A chief tells the braves in which direction to circle the ring the first time, the second time around being hopped in the opposite direction. In this way, each frog will have to hop backward for half of the distance covered.

Keeping balance in this challenge is difficult, especially for the backward frog, and both frogs have to control their hops and positions in order to make the going smooth. The frog who makes the twice-around-the-ring trip in best style and without releasing his hold on his opponent's knees is the winner.

For younger and less seasoned players, the distance may be cut in half by having the frogs hop halfway round the ring, hop around so that their positions are reversed, then continue to the starting point. In this way, each contestant hops backward only halfway around the ring.

To increase the fun, this contest may be staged with two or three pairs of frogs, each frog pair racing against the others. In this event the race is judged from the team viewpoint as well as man-to-man.

POLE GRIP SHIFT

This challenge tests the speed with which a brave can move his hands and his ability to keep calm even when competing against an opponent face to face. Two contestants stand facing each other. The chief gives each of them a lightweight, 4-foot pole, about an inch in diameter. Each holds his pole horizontally at chin level with both grasping the pole firmly at the extreme left end, one hand beside the other.

When the chief calls "Shift!", each contender immediately brings the left hand over the right hand, so that for a moment the pole is held only by the right hand. As the left hand grasps the pole, that hand must be touching the right. The right hand now slips under the left wrist and takes a new grip on the pole, with the right hand touching the left as it takes up its new position on the pole. These movements continue until one hand reaches the extreme right end of the pole.

The chief who judges this challenge must be watchful to

see that one hand really has reached the very end of the pole, because from that point this hand-over-hand challenge continues back to the end of the pole from which the race began. The movements now have to be made in reverse. The brave who finishes first, provided he has made the grip changes correctly, wins.

FAST SNATCH

The winner of this challenge must have quick eyes, agility, and good control of himself. This challenge is really a test of reflexes, as will be seen. It is contested within an area about 15 feet square. The two contestants stand face to face and about 8 feet apart. The chief then ties a short length of white or light-colored crepe paper about 2 inches wide around each elbow of each brave so that only 2 inches of the ends of each strip hang down. Another strip is either fastened behind each player by slipping it through his belt so that only two inches hang down or, when a brave is not wearing a belt, pinning it at waist level with a small safety pin to the back of his breechclout or trousers.

When the chief calls "Attack!", each contender spars lightly with open hands, dodges and evades in order to avoid having his strips snatched while at the same time he tries to snatch his opponent's strips one at a time. Only one strip may be taken at a time and no holding is allowed throughout the challenge. The winner is the brave who first snatches, one at a time, all of his opponent's three strips, while having avoided rough tactics.

TWO-STICK PULL

Cleverness rather than strength or straight pull decides the winner of this challenge. Two contestants sit on the ground facing each other with toes touching. A chief gives them two strong, smooth sticks, each about 14 inches long and an inch in diameter. One contestant holds the end of a stick in each hand. His opponent holds the opposite end of the stick in each hand. The braves must not release either stick during the challenge. A player who does so is considered the loser of that round.

When the chief calls "Pull!", each brave tries to force the other to stand up, by exerting a steady pull on his end of the two sticks. Each tries to avoid being pulled upright by cleverly manipulating the sticks, for instance, by relaxing his pull on one or both sticks when he feels that he is being forced onto his feet. After one challenger has deceived his opponent by some quick work with the sticks, he sometimes finds that it is easy to pull his off-balance rival to an upright position before he has time to resist effectively.

When two braves are equally matched and equally skill-ful, the chief may decide that a near-upright position, instead of a completely upright one, will decide the winner of the challenge. If one of the contestants fails to win within two or three minutes, the result is judged a tie. The best out of three rounds is a good way to decide this test.

HAND SWING

Each brave squats with feet spread apart. They place the palms of their hands flat on the ground in front of them, with knees just outside the elbows. Then they balance forward with their weight on their hands and elbows pressed just behind the knees. They keep their heads back and balance their bodies so that they swing backward and forward between the knees.

On the word "Go," the contestants begin to swing. The one who can do so correctly longest—which will not be for very long—is declared the winner.

UP!

Two or more fellows can contest this feat, which should be judged by speed *and* style.

The contestants sit on the ground in twos, facing each other, and six feet apart. Each brave sits with arms crossed, a hand resting on each shoulder, and legs stretched out in front, with the ankles crossed. On the word "Up!", each contender tries to stand up without uncrossing either his feet or arms. The first brave up who preserves the best balance is declared the winner. Any contestant who uncrosses either arms or legs is ruled out. This contest may be continued until the best at getting up is discovered.

Index

Trailcraft, 108-112
    dangers: 114-116
        animal, 114-116
        plant, 117-120
        snake, 116-117
    emergencies, 112-114
        falls, 113-114
        fire, 112
        floods, flash, 112
        treacherous ground, 113
    enemies, avoiding, 108-110
    trail-blazing, 110-112
Training, Indian boys', 13-14
Transportation, 15-16
Traps, 113-114
Travois, 15
Tripods, 17, 61-62
Trousers, 23
Two-stick pull (challenge), 152-153

U

Up! (challenge), 153-154

V

Vests, 22, 33-34
Vision:
    day, 108
    night, 121

W

War bonnets, 36-38
Wigs, 39-41
Wildlife:
    attracting, 102-104
    finding, 100
    freezing, 99-100
    observing, 98-99
    stalking, 100-101
    tracking, 101-102
    wisdom, Indian, 104-106
Wristbands, 43-44